AF820702

**Advance Praise for *Naked Lens***

"This first-hand, therapeutic approach to video journaling presents an engaging treatise on using a video camera and sites like YouTube as a means for effective self-expression."

—Chad Fahs, Author of *How to Do Everything With YouTube*

"An indispensable guide for anyone who wishes to seize the day by keeping a video diary for self-awareness and healing. Kaminsky has absorbed the wisdom accumulated by centuries of written journal keeping and brought it to the cutting edge mediums of digital video and the Internet. Original, informative and brilliant!"

—Tristine Rainer, Director, Center for Autobiographic Studies
Author of *The New Diary, How to use a Journal for Self-guidance and Expanded Creativity* and *Your Life as Story, Discovering the New Autobiography and Writing Memoir as Literature*

"Yes! The author does a masterful job getting you in the right headspace to be both authentic and creative when you video blog. Can't wait to see how this book affects the online video world."

—Jay Dedman, Author of *Videoblogging*

"This book takes the practice of journaling to a whole new level integrating high tech with high touch. Written in a compelling and easy to understand style that can inspire even the most nontechnical readers to grab a video camera, camcorder or cell phone and begin the eight-week workshop that can change their lives. Sharing individual stories through video journaling has the potential to create a transpersonal evolution of planetary unity and compassion."

—Barbara Ganim and Susan Fox,
Authors of *Visual Journaling: Going Deeper than Words*

"Kaminsky takes the fear out of video journaling and self-expression. This wonderful book proves that it's not the tools we use, but the way we use them."

—LINDA WOODS AND KAREN DININO,
Authors of *Journal Revolution* and *Visual Chronicles*

"Kaminsky brings the art of storytelling into the sacred technology of our times. He reminds us of the many ways we can creatively connect through soulful journaling and self-expression."

—JYOTI, convener of the International Council of Thirteen Indigenous Grandmothers (www.grandmotherscouncil.com), and
Spiritual Director of the Center for Sacred Studies (www.sacredstudies.org)

"I'm a confessed technophobe. Yet this book has me ready to set up my tripod! Terrific applications for a new generation of journal keepers."

—KATHLEEN ADAMS LPC, Director, Center for Journal Therapy,
Author of *Journal to the Self*

"This book is exactly what you need to transform your video presence or wanna-be blog into a truly unique, creative form of self-expression. With Kaminsky as your guide, you can mine the treasures of your unconscious and ignite the muse within, delighting both Jung and Truffaut!"

—DIANA WEYNAND, owner of Weynand Training International (www.weynand.com)
and author of *The Secrets of Video Blogging* and *Final Cut Pro 7*

"Excellent and timely! This inspiring guide helps uncover the storyteller in all of us and leads you through a detailed journey to make those stories accessible on your own terms. It will change the way you think, not only about video, but also about yourself."

—GERALD MCCULLOUCH, Filmmaker and Actor, *CSI: Crime Scene Investigation*

# Naked Lens

## Video Blogging & Video Journaling to Reclaim the YOU in YouTube

Michael Sean Kaminsky

organik media PRESS

Published 2010 by Organik Media, Inc.



Inquiries should be addressed to
Organik Media Press
pr@organikmediapress.com
www.organikmediapress.com



Publisher's Cataloging In Publication

Kaminsky, Michael Sean

Naked Lens: Video Blogging & Video Journaling to Reclaim the YOU in YouTube/Michael Sean Kaminsky

—1st ed.
p. cm.
Includes bibliography and index.

LCCN: 2009911784
ISBN: 978-0-9813188-0-6

1. Digital Video. 2. Blogs 3. Diaries—Authorship 4. Self-actualization (psychology)
5. Creative ability—problems, exercises, etc. 6. Webcasting—Handbooks, manuals, etc. I. Title

# Contents

## Acknowledgments

First and foremost, I'm deeply grateful to Gerry Beekman without whose love, support and endless patience, I might never have finished this book. Thank you very much to my parents, Carl and Sheila Kaminsky, my sister, Laura Kaminsky, and the many friends and colleagues who supported me in countless ways. In particular, I'd like to mention Robert Moeller, who may not be aware of the immense help he provided. I'd also like to thank my editors, Swaha Devi and Denise Leto, as well as copy editor/proofreader Meredith Toillion, who each played instrumental roles in making this the best book possible.

# Part One

# Join the Video Regeneration

# 1

# Introduction

Communicate ideas. Foster creativity. Provoke self-transformation. These are just three ways the written journal (aka the diary) has proven its worth. In the past, journaling meant writing, even if pouring forth one's soul on a laptop computer. Today, inexpensive video cameras and the YouTube phenomenon add a brand-new dimension. For less than the cost of dinner in a fancy restaurant, you can wield a tremendously powerful tool for creativity, communication and self-transformation: The personal video revolution is here.

People tend to approach video from two different but complementary directions:

The personal video revolution is here.

- They video blog—that is, create video for widespread viewing on the Net.
- They video journal—that is, create video for the sake of creative self-exploration (which could either remain private or become a video blog).

In this book we'll explore the role of both. Following are examples of each.

When Hank Green moves from California to Colorado he and his brother John decide to go a full year without any text communication. Instead they video blog to each other. Their entries become the *Vlog Brothers* and are subsequently viewed by millions.

Meanwhile in New York, Claire V. lands her dream job in advertising and wants to capture her feelings. Using a pocket-sized camera, she videos herself in Central Park. Months later she reviews her entries on a rotten day and feels newly inspired. She keeps her video journal private.

Thousands of miles away in England, eighty-two-year-old Peter Oakley (known as "Geriatric1927" on YouTube) sits alone in front of a webcam in his living room. He tells the stories that make up the defining moments of his life and connects with a vast community of all ages beyond anything he ever imagined.

It's impossible to represent the countless ways people use video blogging and journaling in just three situations. We have leapt from the text-based Information Age and landed in the highly visual Social Media Age. Each day people redefine what video looks like, sounds like, and what it means to participate.

Added to the above is the dawning realization that our culture (not to mention planet) seems to be rocketing through its most dramatic shift in recent history. This is apparent on every level from personal to social to environmental. Events in one part of the world have rapid and often unforeseen effects on entirely different locations.

*Don't fight forces. Use them.*

**—Buckminster Fuller**

On the one hand, we are more interconnected than ever. On the other, we are bombarded with media that lacks connection to our lives. This can cause us to shut down on an emotional and spiritual level. Personal video beckons us to abandon the sidelines and re-engage.

Today more people (mainly in the developed world—at least for now) have access to some type of video equipment than at any time in history. Video isn't quite as cheap as a stolen ballpoint pen and the back of a Starbucks napkin, but at this rate, it won't take long. Today anyone can easily create video and deliver it to a massive audience. Yet a surprisingly small number of people take advantage of this potential. For example, according to Internet researcher Jakob Nielsen, less than one percent of YouTube visitors create videos for the other ninety-nine percent who watch.[1]

Not only is video underutilized as a tool for self-expression, it is even more underappreciated as an agent for self-exploration and change. In the past few decades, written journaling has proven its ability to enhance creativity and provoke personal transformation. Video journaling offers similar possibilities as well as its own exceptional potential.

The only requirement is the willingness to leap into new territory. This is less about the so-called "video generation," and more about your own personal video *re*generation.

*Naked Lens* shows how you can use video to:

- → Awaken creativity and inspiration
- → View life from a transformed perspective
- → Conquer camera shyness
- → Increase mindfulness and achieve true on-camera presence
- → Gain a deeper level of self-understanding
- → Create meaningful video blogs that engage viewers
- → Jump ahead of the fast approaching video revolution
- → Connect *self* to *world* with the possibility to change both

*How dare you squander even one more day not taking advantage of the greatest shifts of our generation?*

**—Seth Godin**

If you already record a video blog or journal, the *Eight-Week Workshop* will add an enriching new dimension. If you have *never* videoed yourself but have always secretly wanted to, then read on.

# 2

# Video's "X" Factor

The camera is the mysterious "X" factor.

My first video journal entry remains a vivid memory. It was recorded during a sweltering August heat wave in my insanely tiny Manhattan apartment. The year was 1996 and, not long out of film school, I had moved to New York City from Vancouver, Canada, to check out the indie film scene. I managed to score a rent-stabilized studio just a few blocks from Times Square. It may have lacked a kitchen, but some kind soul had installed two vanities in the bathroom—presumably one for washing dishes. I was as far from the vast, wave-swept shores of the western Canadian coast as you can travel.

I raced up the three flights of stairs to my apartment in what seemed a single breath. It was a Sunday afternoon and I was preparing to shoot an independent documentary the following week. I had just bought a new video camera from a large electronics retailer on the West Side and couldn't wait to try it out.

The tangy chemical aroma of Styrofoam packing and new electronics filled the air. I placed my shiny mini-DV camcorder on its tripod and pointed its lens toward me. I regularly kept a written journal, but because I had the camera, I decided to try something different. I would shoot my first video journal entry.

As I looked into the lens, I felt excited, but also strangely nervous. The nerves caught me off guard. There was no rational reason for my edginess. I'd never felt anxious about writing in my paper journal. Why would I have? But rational or not, I felt a rush of endorphins.

Sweat poured down my brow and stung my eyes. The sweat I attributed to the ferocious humidity and a wheezing air conditioner much too timid to cope with aggressive New York City heat. After all,

I definitely wasn't *that* nervous. Yet the anticipation lingered. I wanted to figure out why.

The video entries were private—or at least I knew that the decision would be one hundred percent mine whether I made them public. There was no reason to feel even slightly anxious. But sitting alone in front of the steady and patient eye of the video camera energized something inside of me.

I pressed the bright red record button and began to speak. As I recorded some of my early experiences and impressions of New York City, the nervousness disappeared. What remained was my curiosity.

I continued to video journal and ended up using one of my entries in an independent documentary I made in 2000 that played the festival circuit. For the most part, though, I kept the majority of my entries private just as with my paper journal. Yet the further I experimented with video journaling the more the idea persisted that there was something special about the experience of speaking directly to a camera.

*All life is an experiment. The more experiments you make the better.*

**—Ralph Waldo Emerson**

Around this time, I came across Julia Cameron's *The Artist's Way*. Cameron's book is a guide for enhancing creativity through written journaling and other methods. This sparked my interest further. I tailored some of her exercises to video. With writing, I sometimes found it hard to get started. With video, the presence of the camera instantly focused me, and I loved the spontaneity. More than once, I found myself speaking about tough times I went through as a kid that I'd nearly forgotten. Whenever this happened it felt cathartic. The words flowed out of me "to" another place—into the camera lens.

Several years later, I started working on TV documentaries for networks ranging from HBO to Sundance Channel. Depending on the project's budget, I sometimes shot interviews on my own. On larger projects, there were three or four crew members. When the camera came on, the emotional intensity inevitably increased with sometimes unpredictable results. It seemed there was more to this than the expected nerves or excitement about being on TV. When the camera rolled, it was as if an unseen energy had suddenly entered the room.

On one occasion, Steve, the subject of a TV documentary, confided that the presence of the camera had compelled him to open himself up to his sister in a way that he'd never been able to before. During their exchange the entire crew blinked back tears, myself included. I had spent time with Steve and the crew beforehand to create a situation where he'd feel comfortable, but the camera was the mysterious "X" factor.

I started to explore this "X" factor in my own life. How could it be used mindfully? What role did the camera play? Meanwhile, I was finalizing the thesis topic for my masters degree and decided to explore the topic in greater depth. I scoured research on autobiographical video and journaling. I made my way through some of the dense texts of media philosophy, searched online blogs, and read magazines and newspapers both online and off.

Media theorists seemed to roughly agree that mainstream media has a potent but not necessarily healthy effect on our psyches. Numerous books explained the technical and creative potential of video blogging. Several academic studies in the field of media psychology outlined the promise that video shows in a diverse range of areas. Finally, a number of excellent books focused on using journal writing for personal growth and transformation.

*We are living through the largest expansion of expressive capability in the history of the human race.*

**—Clay Shirky**

All of the above sources had an important influence on me and they are listed in the *Appendices*. However, there were none that I found that focused on using video for healing or self-exploration. Yet one area that seemed to need healing was our relationship to media.

I began developing a workshop that approached video from this perspective and ultimately wrote this book. My hope is that it serves as a fun and flexible guide to discovering an exciting new approach to video, and perhaps even to life. In the next chapter we'll explore why the power of journaling is a key component to this journey.

# 3

# The Power of Journaling

People use journals for many reasons. They use them to: get to know themselves better, work toward life goals, create a safe place in times of crises, have fun, enhance creativity, preserve history, access the subconscious mind, observe the synchronicities of life, heal the past, get in touch with nature, find spirituality and live fully and deeply within the context of their lives.[1] These are just to name a few. Because they are created by those who keep them, their diversity has infinite potential.

> We meet our reflected selves in a place of color and motion.

In light of the above, journaling poses challenges to the rigid confines of science. Nonetheless, there has been substantial work that shows that journaling is beneficial and even therapeutic. Studies have found that:

- → Journal writing improved overall well-being including mood and general sociability.[2]
- → Daily writing (even just twenty minutes per day) can create a more positive outlook, increase health and improve memory.[2]
- → College students who wrote about traumatic events in a journal went to the health clinic half as much as those who either didn't keep a journal or only wrote about superficial topics. This trend continued to show itself up to four months afterward.[3]

In the world of online journaling, a recent Taiwanese study sampled nearly 700 bloggers and found that those who shared their "experiences, thoughts, and moods through self-disclosure" had greater feelings of well-being. The study concluded that "as the journal blog becomes merged into the user's daily life, it can bring forth many positive benefits through extension of substantial relations, building relations with others, and emotional expression."[4]

Writing (and the written journal) is in no danger of disappearing. However, the video journal offers the infinite opportunity presented above along with a brand-new tool. It's not a question of "instead of" but rather "yes, and now let's see what we can do with *this*."

With the video journal, rather than writing about life events, feelings are expressed to an impartial listener—the camera. There is sound and image. We meet our reflected selves in a space of color and motion. Keeping feelings locked up has been shown to have a range of harmful effects. Expression through speech changes perspective and heals.[5] Further, speaking problems aloud is as beneficial as writing them down.[6]

There is also the opportunity to review our recordings later, and re-experience these moments frozen in time, perhaps from a different perspective. Recent studies have demonstrated that people who were able to review videos of themselves managed to break through negative self-perceptions and reduce their anxieties. For example:

*That sense of failure, I don't know where people put it who don't write songs and aren't able to emote physically. It must go somewhere.*

**—Sting**

- → The University of Manchester had socially anxious teenagers deliver speeches to a video camera. Some had the opportunity to review their performances on tape afterward; others did not. Those given the opportunity to use video feedback found that their negative self-images were inaccurate. In other words—they didn't suck as badly as they thought![7]

- → Teenagers who used video feedback had significant positive changes including reduced anxiety, higher confidence, and more accurate self-perception. Significantly, these improvements remained even when video feedback was no longer provided during subsequent speeches.

→ Supporting the above findings, a study with adults at the University of North Carolina found that video feedback was superior to using "imagining" to correct distorted self-image.[8]

In other words, even though we can envision doing something, it is much more powerful to see ourselves. This doesn't only apply to anxiety-provoking activities such as public speaking. We often hold inaccurate ideas about ourselves, sometimes without being fully aware of them. Video offers the chance to review and revise these faulty self-perceptions.

Creating a video journal reclaims video (and media in general) as an expression of our inner lives. However, video journaling is often colored by people's views of the media, especially television. One critical difference between keeping a written versus video journal is that video involves our physical bodies. In our appearance-obsessed culture some people assume that video journaling isn't much different from sitting in front of a mirror and chatting with one's image. Ignore those people. It's the personal engagement in the process that's important.

*Keeping a journal will absolutely change your life in ways you've never imagined.*

**—Oprah Winfrey**

## —The Myth of Narcissus—

According to one version of the timeless legend of Narcissus, the nymph Echo falls in love with an obnoxious kid named Narcissus who is a complete stud and knows it. If he lived now, he would probably land a modeling gig and be plastered across Times Square billboards. When Narcissus reaches puberty, every boy and girl in his village falls in love with him, but he wants nothing to do with them. Not a single one, out of the entire village. Talk about tough to please!

One morning, Narcissus is alone in the forest hunting deer. Unknown to him, Echo has snuck behind him the entire time. She darts unseen from tree to tree as she struggles to gather the courage to speak. Eventually, Narcissus hears a branch break and shouts out, "Who's there?" Too shy to answer, Echo shouts back, "Who's there?" in response, and this echoing goes back and forth several times until Echo finally shows herself.

Echo walks up to Narcissus and timidly reaches out and holds his hand. She is about to profess her love for him, but he yanks his hand away. He tells her to get lost and tosses in some other cruel things to make it stick. Echo is heartbroken.

One day, the God Nemesis hears poor Echo's cries and decides to punish Narcissus. During his next hunt, Narcissus finds a crystal clear pool of water in the forest and stops to drink. As he leans over the water, he sees his reflection for the first time. (If they had known about mirrors this would be a much shorter story.) He immediately falls deeply in love with the beautiful boy he sees, not realizing that it is himself.

Eventually he recognizes that the image in the pool is his own. Seeing that he will never be able to act on the love he feels, he kills himself. Narcissus's soul is banished to the underworld and Echo plants a flower, thereafter named a narcissus, in the spot where he dies. According to the story, Narcissus still gazes at his image in the murky underworld waters of the river Styx.

*I celebrate myself,*
*and sing myself,*
*And what I assume,*
*you shall assume,*
*For every atom*
*belonging to me as good*
*as belongs to you.*

**—Walt Whitman**

Though some believe that those who video themselves must be falling prey to the same deadly trap as poor Narcissus, it's interesting that people don't tend to have the same reaction to the written journal. There's an implicit understanding that goes along with keeping a written journal that seems absent from video. But there's no reason for this to be the case.

Narcissus looked to his appearance for something that it couldn't give him: a relationship with another person. He didn't have love in his life because he lived a lonely existence and rejected anyone who tried to get close. Keeping a video journal or blog is a way of understanding ourselves so that we can more easily connect with others. This is the opposite of narcissism.

Being unable to encounter your video self isn't humility—it suggests healing is needed on some level. And on the other side, there is nothing narcissistic about being comfortable with the way you look and on friendly terms with your own image.

In the end, as with many activities, it's all about intent. Using video to reach a clearer self-understanding, record for the future, or express oneself is not narcissistic. As you'll find later, many video bloggers gain a better understanding of both others and themselves when they courageously reveal their vulnerability to the world. The video image encourages intimacy and connection.[9]

On the other hand, if you notice a touch of narcissism in you, why not take a look at that as well. Whatever is ignored tends to grow stronger. The more comfortable you are in your own being, the more harmonious your relationship will be with the world.

In the next chapter you'll learn a few of the many other benefits to "being" on-camera.

# 4

# Why Be On-Camera?

Do you remember the first time you saw your image in a mirror as a young child? Perhaps you tried to grab your reflection, laughed, or became frightened. Ultimately, you learned to relax in front of the mirror and simply be. Society imposes assumptions about video (and media in general) that block us from having a balanced relationship with these creative tools. For our purposes, being on-camera is about authentic self-expression and engagement with life.

Following are several key reasons to reclaim video as a tool to *use* rather than be used by.

> Being on-camera is about authentic self-expression and engagement with life.

## —Communicate—

Video is a first-rate lab where you can experiment and strengthen your communication muscles. Every individual has a distinctive perspective and creative voice. Keeping a video journal fine-tunes the part of yourself that feels drawn to help shape the world around you. There are two main reasons this is crucial, one more obvious than the other.

As mentioned prior, there is a massive communication shift occurring and as you'll learn in *Chapter 6*, video is about to be at the dead center of it. Video bloggers often challenge stereotypes if not outright ignore them. For example, Peter Oakley, the eighty-two-year-old video blogger mentioned earlier, was able to break through the often persistent stereotypes surrounding aging.[1] He easily formed authentic connections with people much younger than himself. There are further opportunities to test barriers such as racial and cultural divides. However, this will only happen if there is clarity and creativity of communication.

The less obvious aspect, yet one that's just as important, is the idea of "self-communication." Admittedly or not, most people spend a good part of their day talking to themselves. Of course, if you frequently talk to yourself *out loud* for extended periods in public, you might be granted an unplanned vacation so you can get some "rest." But to talk to yourself silently—through internal dialog—is considered very normal.

Recording a video journal rapidly connects you with the content of this internal dialog. Unfortunately, there is sometimes more jeering than cheering. Yet, alone in front of a video camera, there is generally no live audience. Your audience reflects a part of you. Deep shifts can occur when you become aware of this and change the dialog.

What if you could see yourself a bit more clearly? What if you had the chance to communicate with yourself in a different way? You do have that opportunity—by keeping a video journal. Then you can boldly and effectively communicate in the creative and collaborative conversation of life.

*Man's task is to become conscious of the contents that press upward from the unconscious.*

**—Carl Jung**

## —Explore Yourself—

Ever since Carl Jung promoted the diary as a therapeutic tool, people have journaled as a way to explore their inner selves, uncover deep creative impulses, and heal the soul. Many people carry the heavy burden of unexpressed feelings, emotions, and unstated opinions. As touched on in the prior chapter, unexpressed feelings are one of the primary causes of depression and dampened creativity—unless an outlet is found to release them. When they are released and understood, they can become a source of creative renewal and wisdom.

The video journal presents an ideal opportunity for this release and exploration. You can shout at your camera if you need to and it's unlikely to shout back. If you need to cry, it will be there to record your painful feelings, with the hope of releasing them. When you relay your victories and wild inspirations, it will dutifully record them for posterity. There is no reason to monitor yourself or fear embarrassment—the possibilities are wide open and "delete" is always an option.

## —Play With Identity—

People have experimented with identity on the Internet since its inception. From screen names to multiple online personas, from virtual sex changes to age changes, it's a place where people reinvent themselves.

In the everyday world, you act a certain way, dress a certain way, have a certain job, speak with a certain accent to name just a few of the thousands of elements that differentiate you. Some of these elements are out of your control, like the color of your skin or how tall or short you are, but even with these, you choose how to present them to the world.

Identity on-camera is more flexible than in real life but also subtler and more honest than the old text-based method of screen names and multiple identities. If you have watched video blogs online and think that everyone is the same in everyday life as their postings, think again. People use video to experiment with different aspects of themselves. They wonder what it would be like if they were "X" or "Y." So they create a character with those attributes and try it out.

*I am not my hair I am not this skin, I am not your expectations.*

**—India.Arie**

Experimenting with identity on video becomes a playground that corresponds a bit more closely to everyday life. You can try on a new way of being while you're videoing, enjoy that experience, and slowly incorporate that into daily life. There will be opportunity to explore this further later on.

## —Find Community—

The use of video on the Net revolutionizes the notion of online community. It used to be that online community was kept at arms length from the everyday. This was partly because there was an implicit mistrust. There was no way of knowing who was *really* on the other side of the screen.

But the addition of sight and sound has raised interaction to a new level. Communication is tangible, identity is still malleable, but it is grounded in the real. Communities such as YouTube which emphasize openness and participation may help address issues of social isolation and foster a broader sense of involvement with society.[2] People discover those of like minds and develop a strong sense of connection to one another.

Live video sites such as ustream.com and justin.tv even deliver real-time video feeds directly to viewers' computers or their mobile phones. The concept of online community has grown closer to a true global community of individuals where thousands if not millions of "face-to-face" meetings occur every day. There is virtually no limit to who you might connect with, or where you might travel.

## —Stay Connected—

Most people already use text online to stay in touch with friends and family. Using video is even better. Video chat is available free through many different services. Video sharing sites offer options to make videos private and accessible only to those who you allow to see them.

Like a blog, but more immediate and personal, video gives you the opportunity to remain connected to those you care about. They hear and see your life with a sense of active participation.

*The way we communicate with others and with ourselves ultimately determines the quality of our lives.*

**—Anthony Robbins**

You may find that using video in this way not only brings you closer to your friends or family but that it also wakes up your creative impulses. Because you choose what parts of your life you want to record, you by necessity set priorities as to what is or isn't important. By sharing an inside view with others, your own life may expand in the process.

## —Make History—

Have you ever read a journal entry, email or letter that you wrote a long time ago and wondered to yourself, "Who was that person?" With the passage of time, it can be difficult to relate who you are now to who you were then.

One of the reasons to keep any kind of journal is to keep track of changing perspectives. However, with video there are the hundreds if not thousands of subtle facial cues as well as the tone of your voice, rate of speech, and so on.

Reviewing a video entry weeks, months, or even years later is a powerful experience. You have the chance to meet this "you" from the past face-to-face. This offers an unparalleled window into moments of time. Not only do you experience this for yourself, you have the opportunity to make history for others.

You have probably experienced the thrill of coming across an old letter, journal, or even a holiday greeting card written by a friend or family member who is no longer around. In that moment, it's almost as if they were in the room with you speaking. Perhaps you gained new insight into where you came from as you revisited your roots.

Now you have the opportunity to leave behind a video record for the important people in your life and even the world. Before you protest that you aren't "famous" or "notable," think about this: Some of the most interesting records discovered have been journals or other material regarding the daily lives of so-called everyday people. Consider, for example, Anne Frank who will be covered in the next chapter.

> *I think history is inextricably linked to identity. If you don't know your history, if you don't know your family, who are you?*
>
> —**Mary Pipher**

Everyone plays their part in history. If you don't record your own, the only guarantee is that one day it will be lost forever.

## —Stay Private or Go Public—

Staying private or going public is not an either/or decision. In Taoist philosophy there are two opposing but interconnected forces, the yin and the yang. You've probably seen the symbol to the left which shows their opposite yet interrelated nature. Yin is the nurturing, energy-conserving cycle of existence, whereas yang is the outward manifesting, energy-dispersing cycle. When considering the difference between public and private, this can be a helpful concept to keep in mind.

Neither one is better nor worse, they are both necessary. Energy is built up and restored during the yin stage so it can be released and expressed in the yang stage. Imbalance and disorder occur when one is favored at the expense of the other. Society's current relationship to media appears to be *mostly* yang with *very little* yin.

## Stay Private—Video Journal:

With the written journal, there is an *expectation* of privacy. Though there have been many journals published, generally, when someone keeps a journal or diary, people assume that it's private. For example, if you mentioned to a friend that you were writing in a diary and they responded, "Great, when can I read it!" this would probably be considered a strange request, even from a close friend.

With video, it is the opposite. Mention to someone that you keep a video journal and they'll probably feel that it is perfectly acceptable to say: "Cool! Send me the link!" Nevertheless, it is just as acceptable to keep a private video journal as it is to keep a private written journal. Just as an unpublished diary or journal isn't diminished in value for its author, neither is a video journal less valuable to its creator than a video blog.

Video journaling can be seen as a manifestation of the yin cycle mentioned earlier. The yin cycle is one of creative regeneration and restoration. Your video journals are your sanctuary. By keeping them private, you can relax and experiment with complete freedom. Then, when you feel ready, you can put some of your work out into the world by video blogging. If you never feel ready to go entirely public, that's fine too. As you'll find in the workshop, there are many different ways video can be used for outward self-expression.

*What I come to this for is a little calm. I want to feel connected. I want to not be so isolated and I want also some affirmation of the craziness that I feel...*

**—Jay Dedman, Videoblogger**

## Go Public—Video Blog:

Video blogging can be seen as a healthy manifestation of the Yang cycle. Going public gives you the opportunity to join the growing number of people who actively produce media rather than passively consume it. The more people who reclaim their power to create, the better off our world will be. By communicating and expressing your truth, you inspire others to do the same.

Of course, people video blog for diverse reasons: to entertain, to self-express, to make money, to connect with others, to promote a cause, to teach, to create video art or just to have fun. In the workshop section, we'll explore these reasons further and you'll have the opportunity to decide which ones fit for you.

## —Be a Pioneer—

Were you an early adopter of the Internet or did you play catch-up later? Early adopters began learning and using Internet technologies before they became mainstream. These individuals were pioneers who pushed boundaries—both their own and others'—in experimenting with the new opportunities that arose.

Many early adopters were rewarded financially because they were inspired to launch innovative businesses that had never existed before. Whether profit was a motive or not, all had the opportunity to be part of the vanguard in a massive ongoing transformation of society.

*The real future of communications is video.*
**—Scott Durchslag**

Though the use of personal video has increased over the past years, anyone who begins now is still an early adopter. We have a long way to go and plenty of room for evolution. For example, video is for now mainly watched in a linear way—from beginning to end. Ultimately video will become hyperlinked and interconnected.[3] Small segments of videos will be able to be linked to other small segments.[4] The ability to do this with text led to what we now call the Internet.

This is an exhilarating time not only to join this journey but also to help guide the destination to its highest potential. Our precise itinerary is unknown, but, as you'll learn next if what led us here is any indicator, it will likely be a fascinating voyage.

# 5

# The Road That Brought Us Here

Historically the journal existed primarily as Henry David Thoreau used his—a "daily record of things thought, seen and felt."[1] But to uncover the origins of journaling, we need to travel back prior to the written diary and place video aside for the moment. In fact, we jump to a period thirty thousand years before the Latin word "video" (to see) would even be used, let alone the technology be invented.

We find ourselves in a dim cave. Shadows from a primitive fire flutter against damp rock. One of our early ancestors uses crude stone tools to carve symbols in the cave wall and ochre to color them. On these moisture-laden walls of stone, we view crudely etched images such as: a horse, male warriors, and representations of animals. We may never know the precise purpose behind these ancient artworks, but the fact that they retain such intrigue today points toward their meaning.

> The origin of the journal rose from our innate desire to communicate.

The origin of the journal rose from our innate desire to communicate and express. During the Paleolithic era, when language was a collection of grunts and gestures, we used the most powerful method we possessed. The first "journals" consisted of images.

From nearly as far back as history travels there seems to have been a psychological satisfaction gained from having an audience to communicate one's hopes, dreams, and fears. Whether that audience existed as the damp wall of a cave or brittle sheets of parchment, the experience of communicating held the promise of connection to self and others.

Flash forward thousands of years. Japanese women in the tenth century were among the first to use the written diary as a form of personal expression. These women explored fantasies and internal musings through their private words. Writings such as *The Kagero Diary* laid the foundations for the Japanese literary tradition.[2] But these diaries were accessible to very few people because it wasn't feasible to print books in large numbers.

This state of affairs continued for centuries. Journals and all written works were cloistered among the wealthy and well connected. Then a technology came along that changed the path of history.

Johannes Gutenberg invented movable type via the printing press in the fifteenth century and books were mass-produced for the first time. Once this happened, the information floodgates burst open. The individual who often receives the honor as the first widely published diarist is Samuel Pepys.

Note that what follows is not exhaustive. Visit www.nakedlensbook.com and click "resources" to learn more or to include favorites of your own.

### Samuel Pepys

*Saw a wedding in the church. It was strange to see what delight we married people have to see these poor fools decoyed into our condition.*

—Samuel Pepys

If not for Samuel Pepys, we wouldn't know much about the Great Plague or the Great Fire of London. Yet despite Pepys' eventual fame, when he first began writing his diaries, he intended them to be private—at least at the time. His entries included a combination of personal introspection and eyewitness accounts of great events that might have been lost to history if not for his efforts.

The care Pepys took in the expensive paper he used and the high quality of binding gives a clue that he may have realized that someday someone might find his journals interesting. If that's what he was thinking, he was right. Ultimately, his became the first diary to be published in the 19th century. He probably never realized that he would come to be seen by some as the "father" of the diary and set off a chain reaction that inspired thousands of others to keep their own.

**Takeaway:** What is seemingly "everyday" in your own life might one day be fascinating and valuable to others. However, video has a much shorter life span than paper. In *Chapter 13*, you'll learn how to protect your videos so that they survive as long as possible.

## Lewis and Clark

*This immense river so far as we have yet ascended, waters one of the fairest portions of the globe, not do I believe that there is in the universe a similar extent of country, equally fertile, well watered, and intersected by such a number of navigable streams...*

—Meriwether Lewis

In 1804, the American explorers Meriwether Lewis and William Clark made the first overland journey to the Pacific coast and back to discover the Missouri River area and beyond. In current times no doubt there would have been a feature-length documentary made of their extraordinary journey. If their great trip took place in very recent times, they may have made regular video blog entries and uploaded them to their web page using their mobile phones.

However, Lewis and Clark had to be content with the tools that they had. During their cross-country expedition, they wrote over five thousand pages in a journal that cataloged their experiences as they crossed the continent. Their journal entries often filled dual duties. They were meant both as a record of their travels and as letters to important people in their lives.

**Takeaway:** Consider going beyond the average "travel video" and keep a video journal or blog during your travels. More on how this differs from your regular vacation video can be found in *Week Seven* of the *Eight-Week Workshop*.

## Carl Gustav Jung

*Who looks outside, dreams; who looks inside, awakes.*

—Carl Jung

The first modern psychologist to embrace journaling as a therapeutic device was Carl Jung. He is best known as the Swiss psychiatrist whose therapy sought to help patients understand their psyches by exploring dreams, art, and mythology. Throughout Jung's life, he kept a meticulous and detailed journal referred to as the Red Book because it was bound in red leather. Jung's work on himself and his patients reinforced his view that our main task in life is to discover and fulfill our inner potential.

Jung proposed uncovering our hidden potential by using journaling to explore the unconscious mind. According to his theories, the further the split between the everyday conscious mind and hidden unconscious the less we are able to respond and adapt to life. Dr. Ira Progoff, one of Jung's students, is best known for creating workshops that encouraged participants to explore their unconscious and unveil their inner destiny using a specialized journal format.

**Takeaway:** Video can also be used to tap into the unconscious. In the workshop, there are several exercises that will help you learn how.

**Anaïs Nin**

*So I feel the great changes in the world will come from a great change in our consciousness.*

—Anaïs Nin

Anaïs Nin was a Parisian writer who became famous for ten volumes of her personal diaries: *The Diaries of Anaïs Nin*. Her journals garnered widespread attention not only because of the quality and style of her writing, but because she recorded her active sex life with openness and candor. Today she is considered one of the most influential female authors of the twentieth century.

Nin's ideas surrounding "male" and "female" had substantial influence on feminism. However, the feminist idea of the time that women should be "just like men" bothered her.[3] She strove to use her writing to express and celebrate her true self as an individual (but entirely equal) woman. Nin viewed her journals as an expression of life as art. Ultimately she disassociated herself from the feminist movement believing that self-knowledge gained through *journaling* was the key to personal liberation.

**Takeaway:** Seeing video as an expression of "life as art" can open new channels for self-expression. Learn ways you can translate this into action in *Week Eight* of the workshop.

**Anne Frank**

*I hope I will be able to confide everything to you, as I have never been able to confide in anyone.*

—From the *Diary of Anne Frank*

Anne Frank was born in Frankfurt, Germany, in 1929. Her family was forced to hide from the Nazis in a sealed office flat in Amsterdam after they fled to the Netherlands. Her diary covers two years of her life at that time. Frank's writings are a poignant record of her hopes, disappointments, and conflicts with her family as well as moving observations of daily life.

Frank's diary acted as a cathartic outlet during one of the darkest moments in human history. Frank is also notable for the time she spent looking back at her writing, reviewing it, and reflecting on its meaning. The excellence of Frank's prose and the importance of the subject have led her diary to become the most read of all time.

In Fall 2009, the Anne Frank Foundation created a YouTube channel that includes the only known footage of Frank, as well as the view from her window and the sound of church bells that she wrote about.

Each of the above individuals had an enormous impact on an incalculable number of people. Thousands who might never have kept a diary or journal started because of the influence of these pioneering individuals. But not only that, these diarists were the first in a wave of people who reinforced the value of self-examination. They were the vanguard that showed us that by examining ourselves we could not only enrich our own lives, but the lives of others as well.

**Takeaway:** Looking back at a journal can be as valuable as keeping one. You'll learn about using the "instant replay" in *Week One* of the *Eight-Week Workshop*.

## —The Blog is Born—

During the roughly four hundred years after Pepys popularized the diary, the form evolved dramatically. Many individuals known and unknown adopted the habit of keeping a journal or were influenced by the practice. The early diarists are said to have inspired the "Beat Generation" poet Jack Kerouac's heavily autobiographical novels. Jung's work encouraged individuals to explore their unconscious thoughts and feelings through journaling. Because of Anaïs Nin's impact, the diary became seen as a potentially provocative and liberating act.

But we will never appreciate the true extent of the diarist's influence, because for the many thousands who kept a paper journal or diary, only a small percentage of those were published. Even if someone were keen on making their journal public, it was unlikely they would find a publisher who shared their eagerness. Then in the early 1990s this all changed.

*I believe a blog is a conversation. People go to blogs to read AND write, not just consume.*

**—Michael Arrington**

If you spend time online, you're familiar with blogs. Blogs evolved from the online diary, where people kept a running account of their personal lives. For the first time there were virtually no economic barriers to getting a personal journal out to the masses, no matter how niche the content.

Justin Hall began keeping an online diary in 1994 when he was a student at Swarthmore College and is generally recognized as one of the earliest bloggers. In 1997, an online diarist, Jorn Barger, coined the term "weblog" which was later shortened to "blog." Then in 1999, the Blogger website was launched. It became the first popular, free blog creation service that allowed bloggers to find one another easily—the blogging community was born.

Blogs ultimately changed the face of journalism. Many bloggers cite the "Rathergate" scandal as being the decisive moment when blogs were first taken seriously by the mainstream. In 2004, Dan Rather presented George W. Bush's military records on *60 Minutes*. Bloggers challenged the documents' authenticity and were able to uncover information that proved they were forgeries. CBS had no choice but to make a humiliating public apology. This was a victorious moment for bloggers everywhere. The era of mainstream-dominated journalism was crumbling.

But the history of written journaling and blogging provides only half of our story. In order to continue we need to take another slight detour back in time to the early days of film.

## —The Early Pioneers—

In the classic black and white comedy *Sherlock, Jr.*, Buster Keaton plays a movie projectionist who falls asleep on the job. As he drifts off, he dreams that he becomes part of the film he projects. The movie audience within the film itself and the audience of *Sherlock, Jr.* witness Keaton conjure pure movie magic: He races down the main aisle, leaps up onto the stage, and gleefully enters the film.[4]

*The film of tomorrow appears to me as even more personal than an individual and autobiographical novel, like a confession or a diary...*

**—Francois Truffaut**

Because video is a new technology compared to writing, it may seem that it's only been recently that we've "raced down the main aisle" and leapt into our own videos.

Most people think of the Internet as heralding the revolution of video blogs or video journals. But there are numerous noteworthy pioneering individuals from well before this. The following pre-Internet, and in some instances pre-video, folks laid important groundwork. Though some remain obscure, they are definitely worth checking out. They might inspire you with some innovative ideas and directions of your own.

## Jonas Mekas

Mekas was born in Lithuania in 1922. He emigrated to New York City in 1949 and almost immediately purchased a 16mm film camera. Soon he began recording the moments of his life. Mekas bucked the trend of mainstream Hollywood in the 1960s, and is often credited with inventing the diary film.

His films such as *Walden* have inspired numerous others to explore autobiographical filmmaking. Mekas has kept a film diary of his life in New York since 1950. At the age of eighty-four, he still makes one film every day and posts it to his website.[5]

> **Takeaway:** Creating one video entry per day doesn't need to be difficult. Learn more in *Week One* of the *Eight-Week Workshop.*

*It's available to all and nobody is censoring you. This is a very important change in dissemination. We shouldn't be nostalgic for the past.*

**—Jonas Mekas**

## Ed Pincus

Ed Pincus was one of the first filmmakers to call his work a "diary" in his autobiographical documentary appropriately called *Diaries.* The film includes Ed, his wife Jane, and their two children, and encapsulates the 1970s. Ed and Jane bare both body and soul as they discuss the challenges of their open marriage in intimate detail. He used what was cutting-edge technology at the time to shoot the project entirely on his own.

The innovative film opened the door for others who had big creative visions with small budgets. It also furthered the idea that a diary need not be written.

> **Takeaway:** Deciding to make intimate material public can be rewarding, but it requires consideration. *Week Eight* walks you through various ways of going public.

## Ross McElwee

For over twenty-five years, McElwee has used his own life as a vehicle to explore the grand themes of existence. He is a filmmaker willing to take the risk of allowing a film to be an unpredictable and unplanned process. He often speaks directly to the camera and shoots on his own with the camera placed on a tripod.

In *Sherman's March*, McElwee first sets out to make an essay piece that follows the path of General Sherman, but he undergoes a traumatic breakup just prior to shooting. The film ends up searching for ways to heal a broken heart as McElwee follows General Sherman's path while reconnecting with the women who affected his life along the way. He was one of the first autobiographical filmmakers that showed himself, flaws and all, with boldness and humor.

**Takeaway:** Be open to changing goals and directions. Creating a video blog or journal can throw unexpected opportunities your way.

*I guess to be alone is to know yourself for you and not who you're with—and I like that.*

**—Sadie Benning**

## Sadie Benning

In 1988, fifteen-year-old Benning was home alone one night after having gone through a difficult period. Her father had recently given her a Fisher-Price camera that shot black and white video onto audio cassettes and she began to record her feelings. As Benning expresses it, she liked the fact that "it didn't judge me—it just sat there and recorded what I said." Rather than write in a diary or muse in front of a mirror as many other teens do, she used her camera as a kind of diary-mirror.[6] Benning became the youngest person to be included in the Whitney Biennial. One of her best known works is *If Every Girl Had a Diary*, a video portrait that uses ultra close-ups of her body and surroundings to explore her sexual identity and frustrations with social stereotypes.

**Takeaway:** Learn how you can create your own video portrait in *Week Four of the Eight-Week Workshop*.

### Mark Massi and Tom Joslin

Viewers who watched the final night that *Silverlake Life: The View From Here* was broadcast on PBS witnessed an extremely private moment. They saw the still body of Tom Joslin, who had just died of AIDS-related complications. From behind a shaking camcorder, Tom's partner Mark Massi tells us that Joslin has just died. He then says to Joslin that he loves him and makes a promise to finish the tape.

When the couple was first diagnosed with HIV in the 1980s, it was still a death sentence. Massi began filming a day-to-day video diary of their experiences as they occurred. When Massi died as well, one of his students took the footage and edited it together for broadcast.

> **Takeaway:** Massi and Joslin demonstrated courage in sharing their lives openly and honestly. In *Chapter 14*, you'll learn about some of the ways that people use video blogging to heal and connect.

*Your greatest creation is the life you lead.*

—***Tarnation*** **tagline**

### Jonathan Caouette

Jonathan Caouette created his intensely personal film *Tarnation* from 20 years' worth of primarily self-recorded VHS videotape and old Super 8 footage. He combined these with photographs and answering machine messages to tell the story of his life and his relationship with his mentally ill mother, Renee.

Because the footage was extraordinarily intimate, Caouette had to do some serious soul searching prior to bringing his project to life. It was initially made for a total budget of $218.32, using free iMovie software on a Mac. The distributor eventually spent more to bring the film to theaters, but the film's low budget remains a record.

> **Takeaway:** What aspects of your past might you celebrate or reclaim? You don't need to plan to make a feature film of your life to creatively mine your past.

## —Video Blogging Arrives—

By the year 2000, camcorders had been around for decades and were growing smaller and cheaper each year. In the meantime, the invention of digital video in the late 1990s allowed users to easily and inexpensively edit material on their home computers.

Adam Kontras posted the first video blog (also known as a "vlog") on January 2, 2000. Kontras' video blog was called *The Journey* and it chronicled his move from his hometown in Columbus, Ohio, to strike a path in show business in California. But at that time, few people watched. Not only were there fewer people online in general, but also most people used dial-up connections. Watching video online was an excruciatingly slow and mind-numbing process.

The same year that Adam Kontras made his first foray into online video, Adrian Miles, a researcher at the University of Bergen in Norway, posted his own online video along with a manifesto that detailed his early ideas about video blogging (or "vogs" as he prefers to call them).

*A vog is not streaming video (this is not the reinvention of television).*

**—Adrian Miles**

Three years later, a Brazilian named Nacho Duran posted the first-known South American video blog. It was a diary made up of soundless video loops from a photo sequence he captured with a portable webcam. Early rumblings regarding online video appeared in the media. Ryanne Hodson was profiled by *Business Week* for her "videos that mingle the absurd with oddly touching insights." The Boston radio producer Steve Garfield posted his own video blog online and declared 2004 to be the "year of the vlog."

The media attention continued to build. Though Garfield had beat them to it, *Forbes* magazine jumped on the trend and declared 2005 to be the "year of the vlog" but there were still surprisingly few who were watching and even fewer who actively posted video blogs. For example, the Yahoo! Video Blogging group, formed by video blogger Jay Dedman in 2004, still had just over one thousand members by 2005.

Meanwhile, personal videos began to go "viral." By early 2005 Gary Brolsma's *Numa Numa* video had been viewed over two million times. The video features the rotund and charismatic Brolsma lip-synching and flirting with the camera to what was then an obscure Romanian pop song. Since then it has been viewed an astounding seven hundred million plus times.[7] More importantly it spawned the beginnings of a global community in the form of a mass wave of video responses—thanks to YouTube.

The founding of YouTube increased viewers exponentially and the number of video bloggers and producers of personal video exploded. By 2006, people were watching more than one hundred million videos daily on YouTube according to *USA Today*.[8] *Time* magazine declared "You"—mainly referring to those involved in creating user-generated content online—as their Person of the Year.

Up until this point, the stereotype was that the world of online video was a youthful one. But in 2007, an eighty-year-old grandma "Bubby" was featured in the *Wall Street Journal* for her video blog *Feed Me Bubby*. The video blog was admittedly produced with the help of her grandson, but subsequent seniors went on to produce their own content showing that the movement encompassed all ages.

*You know the cool thing about video blogging? It can be as punk rock as we want it to be.*

**—Michael Verdi**

However, it was in 2008 that video blogging's true impact began to be felt. During the presidential election, video blogs changed the political landscape. Each candidate scrambled to get in the game, ultimately uploading thousands of videos. They had to adjust their strategies once they realized that their mistakes as well as their messages could go viral. McCain learned this the hard way when his "bomb Iran" comment became a YouTube re-mix sensation.

But the viral nature also worked in the candidates' favor. Video bloggers such as musician will.i.am borrowed material from an Obama speech to create a music video called *Yes We Can*. The video became one of the most watched political videos of all time.

Back in 2007, six hours of video were uploaded to YouTube per minute. By 2009, YouTube was receiving one BILLION visits per day and nearly one full day of video was being uploaded per minute according to its owner, Google.[9]

In 2010, Adam Kontras celebrated ten years video blogging with video number one thousand. Meanwhile, many individuals have forged highly successful video blogging careers. In what may or may not be a threat to the movement's grassroots, the entertainment industry has taken note.

The stated goal of YouTube is to have the service "on every screen—to take it from the PC to the living room and the cell phone." Whether it is YouTube that takes us there or one of the many other players, the increased role video will play in our lives seems inevitable. In the next chapter we'll look at some of the ways this is already happening and why this makes the *quality* of our relationship to video as important as available quantity.

*Where the Internet is about availability of information, blogging is about making information creation available to anyone.*

**—George Siemens**

# 6

# Surfing the Video Wave

Everyone who attends school develops their written abilities. It's necessary to gain basic writing skills not only to avoid flunking out, but also to function in the world. However, there is no similar training that teaches people to communicate using video. Younger generations tend to have more experience than older generations, but not consistently. For most, this experience can only be gained by doing for those who are self-motivated. Then there are the few who earn a living in the media, that is, as an actor, newscaster, and so on.

> There is no training that teaches people to communicate using video.

Yet video is becoming part of everyday life so rapidly that it's challenging to keep up. The ability to address a camera with heart and authenticity is an extremely valuable skill to possess. Eventually, those who communicate well on-camera will have a definite advantage over those who do not. It may happen sooner than you think.

Ten years ago, who would have thought that we would ditch our landlines in favor of mobile phones? Who could have predicted that blogging would transform journalism? Who could have imagined that we would be "tweeting" to one another or that we would exchange intimate personal details and photos on a service called Facebook?

Picture all the above but toss in a video component, not just as an add-on, but as an integral part. This shouldn't be tough to do because it is already happening. This gives a taste of where we are likely to head in the next few years—but just a taste. It doesn't include all the inventions we can't imagine because no one has invented them. . .yet.

**Consider this:**

- → Videophone technology has been around since the 1970s, but now it is poised to take off big time. Many cell phones already record video. There are rumors that one major mobile phone manufacturer plans to turn its phone into a mobile video conferencing device in the near future.

- → Chatting has changed. For roughly ten years, chatting online has meant text, but no longer. Tools that have built-in video capability such as Skype, iChat, and Google's Wave platform are transforming what it means to chat.

- → Video conferencing was once confined to certain industries due to cost. With a camera built into every laptop and the numbers of telecommuters rising each year, video has become essential to a variety of businesses and its usage is increasing.

- → "Telepresencing" uses high-definition video and multiple LCD screens to emulate physical presence. Corporations are the primary users due to its expense. Nevertheless, like all technology, it will fall in price and find its way to home users. With 3D TV now a reality, 3D telepresence will no doubt follow.

- → Video résumés are requested with increasing frequency. Employers want to save time and have a "face-to-face" meeting before they meet in person. As cost-cutting becomes the norm, this will likely increase.

- → Colleges such as Michigan State University now accept video submissions as a supplement to the traditional personal statement. At some point this may become a requirement.

*When it comes to the future, there are three kinds of people: those who let it happen, those who make it happen, and those who wonder what happened.*

**—John Richardson Jr.**

- Small business promotion, social activism, and personal branding are three more areas that already use online video and will only see that opportunity grow in the coming years.

- It is now easy to post live video online from a mobile phone. This poses a threat to broadcast news in the same way blogging challenged the newspaper industry. The many other ways this will change everyday life have yet to be seen.

Email changed communication. The speed of information increased exponentially. This has offered incredible opportunities as well as some challenges. Mainstream culture's relationship to media, especially visual media, is not altogether healthy. Yet change rushes forward. Now it is up to you whether change happens because of video or whether you use video to *create* change. In other words, you can fight forces, or you can use them—to transform your own life and potentially those of others.

Are you ready? Let's choose the best tool for you.

*The most profound technologies are those that disappear. They weave themselves into the fabric of everyday life until they are indistinguishable from it.*

**—Mark Weiser**

# Part Two

## Getting Started

# 7

# Choose Your Tools

The tools required to keep a video journal or video blog are minimal. In the following section I've deliberately stayed away from naming specific equipment models wherever possible. These tend to change every few months. On the www.nakedlensbook.com website, I've included some helpful tips and places to go for further information. If you already have a camera you love, feel free to skip ahead to the next chapter.

> The tools required are minimal.

## —Video Camera Selection—

Cameras can be large or tiny, complex or straightforward. But the quickest way to dive in is to start with what you own. Once you have a better idea of your needs, you can always upgrade. What follows is a brief rundown of the most popular options. Compare them with what you already have.

### Built-in Laptop Cameras:

If you own a current laptop, you may already have a camera included as part of the package. They are usually embedded in the screen casing in the top center.

Built-in cameras are a decent option and work well for keeping a basic video journal or video blog. Remember, though, that because it is fixed to your laptop your mobility will be limited. Laptops come in all sizes, so presumably you could lug a laptop around if you wanted to shoot on the go, but it wouldn't be super convenient.

## Digital Still Cameras:

If you own a digital still camera, it likely shoots video with sound as well. The image can vary from quite basic up to "HD" (high-definition) in quality. If you want a low-cost way of keeping a journal for personal use or even to post online, this option can't be beat for cost and portability.

The downside is that digital still cameras often lack sound quality. The microphones tend to be tiny and badly located on many models. This leads to "tinny" sound and unavoidable handling noise when you move the camera around. In addition, if you don't already own a small tripod you may ultimately want to buy one. A tripod will make recording your entries much easier.

## USB Web Cameras:

*The video cameras are so cheap and so are Internet connections, we're heading to a place where even the most casual of encounters may be captured and broadcast.*

**—Dave Winer**

Many people own a small USB web camera that is separate from their computer. You might remember the eyeball-shaped Logitech "Quickcams." These were the first widely available web cams and Logitech still manufactures a range of these devices today. If you own an older model the resolution may be on the low side but it should be fine for basic use. If your camera is so ancient that it only shoots black and white, the resolution is probably low enough that your own mother wouldn't recognize you. Keep it as a collector's item and pick up a new one.

Webcams have advantages in that they are extremely convenient and always ready for use. Because they're tethered to a computer, it's difficult to change camera angles or rove about. Wireless Bluetooth cameras help to work around this limitation somewhat.

## Camcorders:

Camcorders come in numerous varieties. They can be palm-sized (or even smaller) devices that record directly to memory or larger "video cameras" that record to videotape, memory, hard disk, DVD or

Blu-ray disks. In general, no matter the size of the camera, the trend is away from tape or disks toward solid-state memory storage.

With higher end camcorders, you have the widest range of options for adjusting the image and sound to your liking. Since they're portable and not tied to your computer, you can pick them up and take them with you—giving you the option of recording yourself nearly anywhere.

### High-definition vs. Standard-definition:

One important influence on the quality of a video image is the number of pixels contained per inch. High-definition (HD) has many more pixels per inch than standard-definition (SD). Greater numbers of pixels equal more visual information included in terms of the image's color, luminosity, and motion. The more visual information in the image, the closer it is to what your eyes see in real life.

Camcorders vary widely in price. Generally, the standard-definition cameras are lower priced than high-definition. That said, HD grows less expensive every month. So how does someone choose?

*Any sufficiently advanced technology is indistinguishable from magic.*
**—Arthur C. Clarke**

You don't absolutely need HD to record a video journal or to put up a video blog. On the other hand, HD is now common online. Not only that, if you want to lower your video to standard-definition (or less) to reduce the file size, it's easy to do with the right software. But you also have the option of using full HD if you like. (It's possible to do it the other way as well—convert SD to HD—but the results vary because the computer needs to "fake it" by adding visual information that wasn't actually recorded.)

Ultimately, standard-definition as a video camera format will disappear completely. If you decide to purchase a camera, it won't cost you much more to spring for HD and this gives you the option to shoot in either format. To sum this all up, my advice would be to purchase HD if you don't already own a camcorder. If you currently own an SD camera you can easily make do for a while as you watch HD cameras grow cheaper by the month.

### Mobile Phone—Moblog Posts:

Would you, could you in a boat? Just as Sam suggests in Seuss' green eggs and ham, with the right mobile phone you can shoot anywhere. Using a mobile phone to record video is handy when moving around and you'll always have your camera with you. Phone camera quality continues to improve and opens up the possibility for spontaneous entries in all sorts of random places. Some models even allow you to shoot live video and post directly to the Net.

### Tape vs. Tapeless:

There are several ways to record video:

- Onto tape (in most cases MiniDV or HDV tape).
- Directly to solid-state memory (such as an SD card—the thumbnail-size memory cards common to digital still cameras).
- Directly to a DVD or Blu-ray disk.
- Onto a hard drive.

*Say! I will eat them ANYWHERE!*

**—Dr. Seuss**

Tape-based camcorders still sell, but we are headed for a tapeless world in the near future. However, whatever current format you choose (even tape), it is all *digital* video.

Of the above recording methods, I generally advise against those that record directly to DVD or high-definition Blu-ray disk. These are fine if you simply want to archive what you shoot or show the videos to friends and family. But if you want to edit the material or post it online, the process of converting a DVD or Blu-ray requires an additional step to prepare the footage.

In general, recording tapeless offers many advantages. With tapeless you can transfer your digital movie files from camera to computer quickly. Images recorded to tape require a transfer that takes place in real time. In other words, one hour of recorded footage takes one hour to transfer. Additionally, there are fewer moving parts in tapeless cameras so they tend to be light and reliable.

If you use an older (dare I say ancient) camera that records to tape formats such as 8mm, Hi8 or VHS, you will be recording *analog* video, not digital. Technical issues aside, this means that if you want to edit, upload, or store the material on your computer, it needs to be converted to digital form. This usually involves buying an analog-to-digital convertor for your computer.

These cameras have become obsolete so it won't be an issue for most people. But if you do happen to own one, consider purchasing a camera that shoots in a digital format. Buying the analog-to-digital conversion equipment will be an additional cost. By the time you purchase this, you might as well have purchased a new camera.

*Style used to be an interaction between the human soul and tools that were limiting. In the digital era, it will have to come from the soul alone.*

**—Jaron Lanier**

### Testing—one, two, three:

Audio is an important component of video that people sometimes overlook. Part of the charm and immediacy of personal video can be rough images and sound. But the charm only goes so far. In general our eyes are much more forgiving than our ears.

When you watch videos that are pixelated, have jerky camera movements and offbeat framing, your visual cortex "fills in the blanks" and you barely notice. In fact, these videos can be a refreshing break from the onslaught of mainstream, highly produced media. On the other hand, if every second word is garbled or there is so much background noise you can't understand what is being said, you're going to click onto something more interesting.

But what if you never plan to make your videos public? Does quality matter then? Most people have had the experience of coming across an old letter or written journal entry with missing pages or indecipherable handwriting. I've wrestled with my own handwriting from old journals I'm sorry to admit. It's just as disappointing to look back at a video entry months or years from now and discover that you can't understand your own words. Not only that, clear audio increases the presence and intimacy of your recording.

### Microphone Considerations:

Whatever microphone comes with your camera is most likely fine for general use. Keep in mind that the farther away you are from the mic, the more distant you'll sound. This can come across as a rather hollow quality that can change the emotional tone of the recording.

If you use your computer to video yourself and want a warmer, more intimate tone, consider buying a separate mic. This allows you to position the mic so that it's closer to your mouth and provides better sound. Computer mics come in many different configurations. Some clip onto the laptop or side of the monitor, others sit mounted on the desk or you can purchase a headset.

A microphone headset is practical if you want to leave your hands free. It also provides sound that is even and reliable since the mic remains the same length from your mouth at all times. On the downside, since you'll also be recording the visuals, you'll need to look at yourself with the headset on. Speaking from personal experience, my headset gave me disconcerting flashbacks of a short-lived career telemarketing water coolers during college, but this is really a matter of personal taste. Buy a headset from a local electronics chain and try it for a few days so you can return it if it ends up bugging you.

*I have always thought it would be a blessing if each person could be blind and deaf for a few days ...Darkness would make him appreciate sight; silence would teach him the joys of sound.*

**—Helen Keller**

If you're using a camcorder, you'll either use the onboard camera mic or plug in a higher-quality external camera mic if your model has mic inputs. This mic will be different from the computer mics mentioned above. Most mobile phones and digital still cameras do not have inputs for external mics.

## —Computer Selection—

If you already own a computer, whether it's Macintosh or Windows-based has little bearing on what you can accomplish. Software availability differs between the two (although Macs manufactured with the Intel chip can run Windows and thus many Windows software titles) but there are plenty of options for both. There are also less common alternatives in terms of operating systems such as Linux, but if you are technically savvy enough to have chosen Linux, you don't need my help in figuring out your video options.

If you don't own a computer or intend to upgrade, the decision is a matter of your comfort level. Are you already familiar with either Mac or Windows? Then that should be a consideration (unless you love to learn new things). Either platform allows you to video journal, video blog, and edit videos as needed. There are websites that spend pages arguing this topic, but for our purposes it's not necessary to discuss in detail.

*Computing is not about computers any more. It is about living.*

**—Nicholas Negroponte**

If your goals veer toward a more complex project involving extensive editing, then the Mac may have an edge because you can use Final Cut Pro (professional-grade editing software) to work with your material. To be fair, I use a Mac myself so I'm admittedly biased.

Perfect. Now you have everything you need to begin shooting. However, when the time comes to look back at your videos, if you can't find half of them, you'll be in for a frustrating experience. Up next is a quick chapter that will help you avoid this.

# 8

# Stay Organized

One of the challenges to keeping a video journal or blog is the ability to catalog your material. The benefits and rewards of journal-keeping increase the longer you do it. If you record yourself for just ten minutes per day, this will add up to a substantial amount of material over time.

If you used a word processor to keep a written journal and you were interested in looking back at a certain life event, you could easily perform a text search to find the entry.

> The benefits and rewards of journal-keeping increase over time.

For video material, it can be either extremely frustrating or refreshingly simple depending on how you set it up. Following are some basic techniques to help keep your video organized. These will also be useful if you decide you want to create a larger project that spans several different time periods.

To organize this ultimately large, not to mention precious, amount of material, it's easiest if we start from the beginning. The most basic information that should be included with every entry is the date and time it was recorded. Depending on the equipment you're using, this can be done in a few ways.

If you own a camera that records directly to solid-state memory or hard disk, skip ahead to the *Tapeless Organization* section following. If you use a tape, DVD or Blu-ray based video camera read on.

**Tape/Disk Based Organization:**

Mark your videocassettes or disks with the date of your first entry and then the final entry when the cassette or disk is full. Put this on the media and the case itself (but definitely label both—I know from experience that it's extremely easy for tapes to become separated from their boxes). If you feel especially creative, you can make the cases themselves miniature works of arts—color them, doodle on them, and so on. Don't attach anything that could fall off and become jammed in the machine though. That would not be fun.

Proper labeling creates a broad but useful guide to your material. However you will likely have *many* entries on one tape or disk. There are two general strategies that can help keep things organized. One is filling out a log that lists various details about each entry. A sample log is provided at www.nakedlensbook.com for download.

The second thing you can do—though only useful in certain situations—is to set up the date/time function on your recorders so that each entry has the date/time "burned" into it. This means the date and time will be electronically (and permanently) recorded onto the media itself.

The advantage to this is that the entry will never become separated from the date and time it was recorded. The disadvantage is that if you decide to use the material for another purpose—for example a video blog online or other project—you will be stuck looking at the burned-in times. Additionally, you might decide to edit together a longer project and prefer not to have the date when the previous material was shot displayed. Burn-ins lack flexibility.

*Organizing is what you do before you do something, so that when you do it, it is not all mixed up.*

**—A.A. Milne**

Some recorders include "metadata" (data that is included on the tape but not burned onto the video image itself) which bypasses the above issue. If you have this option I definitely recommend it over burned-in date/time. With some cameras, you can customize the data so that each entry includes a specific name or date of your choice. Every camera is different though. Check out your camera's instruction book under "metadata" or web search your camera model plus "metadata" to delve into this further. If you decide to use burned-in dates/times or metadata, I still recommend keeping a log so you can add an extra layer of info such as a description.

Though your camera records to tape, DVD or Blu-ray disk, you will still likely want to transfer some or all of the footage onto your computer at some point. This leads us to the tapeless segment of our process.

## Tapeless Organization:

If you use a camera that records directly to a tapeless digital format, your job is somewhat easier. You should name each file with the date and time. This is the default mode for some cameras. Even though computer filenames automatically insert date and time, these aren't necessarily reliable since they may change during the process of backing up a file or when you re-open it. If you are transferring footage from tape or DVD/Blu-ray disk, then be sure to name your files once they are on your hard drive.

**For example: 2012-12-21-430pm.mov.**

There are certain characters such as forward and backslashes that aren't allowed in a computer filename. You may also want to add a couple of words that describe the entry. I recommend putting the date first, then a brief description. This will make it much easier to search later. Make sure you choose one convention and stay consistent. This way you will be able to sort and search with ease.

*Productivity is being able to do things that you were never able to do before.*
**—Franz Kafka**

**For example: 2012-12-21-430pm-newjob.mov.** This could describe an entry where you vent your feelings about a new job.

Using the above method you can also create an electronic file log that includes more detailed information. Using a program such as Microsoft Excel or the free spreadsheet software included in the downloadable Open Office you'll have a searchable record of all your video entries.

## Video Blogging Software:

There is software specifically created to help in the video blog process. Whether or not this software will be useful to you will depend on what your ultimate goals are for your material. Video blogging software offers features such as teleprompters if you plan on reading from a prepared script. They also offer some helpful ways of organizing a daily video blog and getting it up on the Internet.

Following are two examples of software packages.

***Adobe Visual Communicator PC ONLY***

Adobe Visual Communicator (VC) is the main option that replaces the discontinued Adobe Vlog it!. VC has everything you need to make a "professional" looking video blog, though it is slightly more oriented toward a news look and feel.

Visual Communicator includes digital replacement of your backdrop (more on this in the *Eight-Week Workshop*) a built-in teleprompter and a template that remembers the format of your last video entry so you can quickly record a daily video blog. It also provides the capability to shoot segments out of sequence and edit them together without re-recording the entire video.

*The real danger is not that computers will begin to think like men, but that men will begin to think like computers.*

**—Sydney J. Harris**

***Videocue (Telestream) MAC ONLY***

Videocue is a solid platform for creating and organizing your video entries. It integrates with online blogging sites such as LifeJournal and Blogger. Similar to Visual Communicator, it includes a range of graphics and a robust teleprompter function.

Both Videocue and Visual Communicator offer free trials at the time of this writing. I strongly recommend that you try before you buy to see if they are something you really need.

Next in *Part Three*, you'll choose the best time and place to record your videos and learn the one thing to do to get the most out of the *Eight-Week Workshop*.

# Part Three

## Lights, Camera, Action!
## The Eight-Week Workshop

# 9

# Before You Begin

Video journaling is still somewhat unexplored territory. The exercises that follow offer the opportunity to engage in a form of self-exploration you may not have experienced before. There are many benefits to this, but don't underestimate the intensity of taking this video journey.

If an exercise takes you somewhere you aren't ready for, then back off and proceed slowly. If painful issues emerge that you aren't prepared to deal with on your own, please seek outside help such as a licensed therapist, spiritual counselor, or your doctor. Be gentle with yourself!

> Your mission is to make one video entry every day.

## —Eight-Session Overview—

For the next eight weeks, your mission is to make one video entry every day. At the beginning of each week, read the exercises for that week from start to finish. Feel free to skip some exercises or do others more than once over the course of the seven days.

You'll also likely come up with ideas of your own along the way. Experiment with these as well. This is your workshop. If you come up with an exercise you'd like to share, please visit the website specifically created for the workshop at www.videoregeneration.com.

Whatever you might change or add of your own, one thing that *is* important to the overall experience is to make one video entry every day—even if it is very brief. When time is limited, I recommend at minimum doing the two-minute warm-up that you'll be introduced to next, called the "daily check-in."

### The Daily Check-in:

The daily check-in is a two- to five-minute, completely free form entry. It could be about absolutely anything. It's a great way to wake up the creative self and is also an ongoing and unfiltered record of what's on your mind. It is comparable to a method called "Active Imagination."

Active Imagination is a technique that Carl Jung used to "dialog" with his unconscious mind. Active Imagination gives the opportunity to release judgment and allow the inner-self free reign. It can be done using visualisation, writing, painting, and many other ways, but in this case, we'll use video.

Some prefer to do a "stream-of-consciousness" type of exercise such as this one in the morning. The logic behind a morning exercise is that the conscious mind is still half-asleep, allowing the opportunity to tiptoe past the internal censor and connect to deeper wisdom. Having just woken up, there also may be lingering dream imagery to explore. You might try it during several different times of the day and see which works best for you. You'll learn more about the check-in during *Week One.*

*Our life is composed greatly from dreams, from the unconscious, and they must be brought into connection with action. They must be woven together.*

**—Anaïs Nin**

## —Create the Ritual—

Magic occurs when we make something a daily ritual. When something becomes part of daily routine, a natural momentum gathers. Not only that, when the videos are reviewed there will be a wide range of material to learn from or to make use of in any way that inspires.

When it comes to journaling, people tend to fall into one of two groups. The first group makes entries when life is great and they are in the right mood. When life is less than perfect, they lack the motivation.

But when they push through and record even on the days they don't feel like it, they may find that they are rewarded many times over. First, the sheer act of expressing feelings on-camera can change them. Second, when the entry is reviewed, perceived problems can be considered with fresh eyes.

The second group of people tends to video when life drags them down. When life is fab, they don't have the time. Or they don't have much to say. Sometimes it's easier to express the tough times in life than it is to celebrate the positive.

People who fall into this category block themselves from experiencing the rich tapestry created by keeping a video journal through all the cycles of life. The review stage can also be a downer for this group as they may wonder if they are ever happy. If either of the above describes you, it's important to decide on a consistent schedule and stick to it.

## —Time and Place for Everything—

Maintaining any new activity on a daily basis can be daunting. But it doesn't need to be. On a busy day, your entry could consist of a quick warm-up and a five-minute shoot. Allow another few minutes for set up and to catalog your entry, but we're only talking ten or fifteen minutes total. Much can be gained in one short entry.

*Happiness within a diary has less to do with the events you encounter in life than with the way you experience the process of living.*

**—Tristine Rainer**

Scan the week ahead and see if you can find openings where you can set aside a specific time. Maybe you can even sneak an entry on a work break. I won't tell. Remember, though that files stored on work or school computers should never be considered private. Keep your video safe on the camera storage until you get home.

A video blogger by the name of Ravi Jain even recorded a regular video blog from his car. He called it *Driveaway* (you can still find episodes online). It eventually evolved to include call-in interviews! Video and driving tend not to mix when you're the one behind the wheel, but in some cities stop-and-go traffic is a lot more "stop" and a lot less "go," so this is your call.

Finally, is there a quiet place in your home where you can video? Will you need to setup a special place or make an agreement with your housemates? Having an established location where you feel comfortable and won't be interrupted is important. Consider the aesthetics of your location. Is there enough light? Your set-up doesn't need to be extravagant, but it should be something you find harmonious to your eyes.

All right, enough talk. Let's begin!

*Week One Notes:*

10

# Your Video Regeneration

## Week One

### Befriend the Naked Lens: Overcoming First-Date Jitters

Do you have your camera out and ready? Are you happy with the place you've chosen to record yourself? This first exercise starts with something that is often overlooked but important: a quick physical warm-up.

When you see the ✪ symbol visit videoregeneration.com for a video demo of the exercise.

#### ✪ Get Physical ✪

Folks who make their living in front of the lens often go through numerous warm-up exercises before they appear on-camera. They know that tension in their bodies shows up as tension in their faces, voices and in how they carry themselves. The physical is the gateway to the emotional, and when the body is locked up, nothing will escape.

A well-studied technique called progressive relaxation is a simple method to calm mind and body. You can do it wherever you are right now.

First, take several deep "three-part" breaths. Three-part breathing is a type of deep yogic breathing that infuses air into all the tiny pockets of the lungs. It was taught to me by a respected Yogi and Buddhist monk named Bhante Rahula at a retreat center in West Virginia. Many people breathe shallowly either in their mid-chest or belly. Yogic breathing floods your body with oxygen.

- First, place one hand on your belly. Breathe in through the nose and feel your stomach expand.
- Next, place your hand on your mid chest (near your sternum). Concentrate on feeling this area expand as you breathe in.
- Finally, place your hand on your upper chest (two inches below your neckline) allowing the air to flow into this area. It can take practice to feel full expansion in the upper chest, as we don't often breathe this deeply.
- Now, put all of the above together in one smooth breath. Breathe into your stomach, then mid chest, then upper chest. This is a three-part breath.
- Release the breath through your nose and mouth to the count of seven.
- Repeat this a few more times and notice the sensations of relaxation.

*For breath is life, and if you breathe well you will live long on earth.*
**—Sanskrit Proverb**

You'll be much more relaxed on-camera and in life if you remember just this one practice. Breathing through the nose stimulates the parasympathetic nervous system. This is the part of the nervous system responsible for calming you down. This leads to muscle relaxation, lowered heart rate and reduced blood pressure.

Have you taken a few yogic breaths?

- Now, tense your feet—curl your toes as tight as you can, and take a three-part breath.
- Let the breath out, release the tension in your feet, and allow your muscles to relax.

- ✦ Don't forget to make some noise. It can be a long and easy "aaah" sound, a menacing growl, an extravagant sigh or whatever feels natural.

Continue this tensing and releasing all the way up the body remembering to focus on your:

- ➜ Feet
- ➜ Calves
- ➜ Thighs
- ➜ Buttocks
- ➜ Pelvic Area *(focus on the muscle you tighten when you really "gotta go")*

*Tension is who you think you should be. Relaxation is who you are.*
**—Chinese Proverb**

- ➜ Stomach
- ➜ Chest
- ➜ Arms
- ➜ Hands
- ➜ Shoulders
- ➜ Neck
- ➜ Face *(scrunch your face up as tightly as you can and then let go)*

Finally, we'll do a quick vocal warm-up. Warming up the voice increases self-expression. A lackluster monotone sucks meaning from even the most important issues. Watch the political TV network C-Span for a few hours if you need proof.

✦ Massage the point of your jaw beneath your earlobe. It's the place where your jaw opens and closes (the temporomandibular joint). Gently open and close your mouth as you do this.

✦ We store lots of tension in our jaws. Releasing these muscles helps deliver clear and expressive speech.

✦ Massage your throat area gently and make a humming sound as you pass air through your lips.

In Eastern healing traditions such as Ayurveda, the throat is the site of communication. Places where energy concentrates are better known as chakras. Massaging these areas increases energy flow and releases blockages and tension.

*Self-expression must pass into communication for its fulfillment.*

**—Pearl S. Buck**

✦ While humming a steady tone, allow your lips to vibrate in a "raspberry" of titanic proportions. Consider backing away from delicate objects (and finicky pets) when you do this.

Remember to do these exercises before each entry. Create your own abbreviated version if you like or perhaps extend them and spend longer. You can never be too relaxed—unless you fall asleep. Definitely avoid that. It doesn't make for riveting video. This warm-up should leave you relaxed but invigorated.

## —Video Virgins—

If you've never spoken one-on-one to a camera before, the first time may feel awkward. Don't rush this exercise, and have fun without taking yourself or the activity too seriously.

It might sound odd right now, but there's a unique relationship that will steadily develop between you and the camera. Though this is really more about a new relationship you will develop with yourself, making an introduction provides the perfect, non-threatening place to start.

Put your camera on something stable (depending on your set-up this may be a tripod—or the camera may already be fixed to your laptop or attached to the computer). Turn your camera on and make sure that it's recording properly.

Experiment with different positions. Move farther away or get closer to the lens. If you're sitting, try standing up. You might even lounge on your couch or bed and hold the camera above you. Go with whatever feels comfortable.

*The secret to a rich life is to have more beginnings than endings.*
**—David Weinbaum**

Each decision has its impact and we'll explore these in depth later. For now, enjoy experimenting without worrying about what it looks like.

### •••Shoot•••

✦ Introduce yourself. Start with basic information such as your name, age, and where you live.

✦ Get detailed. What are some of the things that you often tell people when you first meet them? Give your mini-bio.

✦ Incorporate one thing that you usually *don't* tell people when you meet them, but that you wished you mentioned more often.

✦ Share your goals for starting this video journal. What do you hope to gain from it? What would you like to see occur over the next eight weeks?

Pay attention to moments when you feel uncomfortable or suddenly run out of things to say. Make a mental note of what triggered them for exploration later.

## —The Daily Check-in—

The Daily Check-in is your chance to make a free-form entry on whatever you like. For this first week, you began with the above introduction, but from now on I recommend doing your check-in before starting the exercises.

Do your check-in as the pure stream of consciousness mentioned prior. Here is your opportunity to release all judgments and let it flow. This is a simple technique, but the tendency is for the conscious mind to turn it into something complicated. Try and avoid this. There is no need to plan or analyze.

*Everything becomes a little different as soon as it is spoken out loud.*

**—Hermann Hesse**

### •••Shoot•••

- ✦ Hit record and make a completely unstructured entry. Think of the daily check-in as a "brain drain" and let it all hang out.

- ✦ If you find that you have nothing to say, say something anyway! Talk about how it feels to draw a complete blank. Ask questions to get yourself started—but keep them small and specific. For example, "What's been one unique thing about my day so far?"

- ✦ Try to make your daily check-in at least two minutes no matter what.

There is often more than we realize waiting to be spoken. Big, general questions tend to freeze us up, whereas simple, specific questions activate the brain.

## —Instant Observations—

It's important to stay grounded on-camera. Otherwise, it's easy to become "lost" in the eye of the lens and lose focus. The following exercise brings you into your present environment and wakes up perception. This is key in fostering creativity and spontaneity.

### •••Shoot•••

- ✦ Start with where you are: home office, living room, bedroom, kitchen, or even coat closet. These will all work great.

- ✦ Close your eyes and take one or two three-part breaths. Gently roll your neck from side to side.

- ✦ Now open your eyes and describe the first object that you see. Don't analyze, just go with your first impulse. Trusting instinct fosters freedom and creativity.

*If you observe well, your own heart will answer.*

**—Rene A. Schwaller de Lubicz**

Once you've described what you see, let your eyes travel around the space. Ask the seemingly obvious question: "What am I seeing?" We often see without perceiving, especially in a place we know well. Look for unnoticed details—texture, color, shadow, reflection, unappreciated beauty, and whatever else enlivens your eyeball.

- ✦ Close your eyes again but leave your camera running. When you open your eyes, see if there are *still* new details you can find despite your efforts just moments earlier. There are millions of details hidden everywhere. It's just a matter of a shift in attention.

- ✦ You might be tempted to move the camera and show your discoveries, but this defeats the purpose for now. The goal is to describe what you see and bring it to life using your words, voice, gestures and facial expressions.

## —Video Fright—

Feeling nervous on-camera has parallels to stage fright but also differences. If you try the above exercises over a few days and can't relax, you may have some form of "video fright."

In classic stage fright, the physical presence and live aspect of the audience creates a fear of both failure and judgment. One early theory put forth by psychologist H.L. Hollingworth, proposed that stage fright resulted from two opposing instincts—the "craving" to have an audience conflicting with the fear of a crowd.[1] But when you are alone with your camera, the only audience present is the one created in your own mind. The only person judging you is yourself. Years ago, I learned this the hard way.

Just out of high school I decided it would be fun to host a travel show for teens. The city I lived in had a public access station and I applied with my proposal. They gave me a slot and I was thrilled. A man I had worked for during the summer owned a production company. He taught me how to use his editing equipment. I borrowed a tall stack of National Geographic documentaries from the library and spent hours editing a snazzy show opening.

*Fear is a darkroom where negatives develop.*

**—Usman B. Asif**

The day of my first show I was a little nervous, but felt well prepared. Because it was public access, shows were recorded live to tape in real time. No opportunity for mistakes.

I walked into the studio. The set was simple, neat, and pristine. Surrounding this oasis of calm was a tangled jungle of cables and equipment. A very patient man gave me basic instructions while another put a mic on me. I sat on-set and watched the count through the control room window. Five, four, three, two... The red light on the main camera illuminated.

I was "live." But inside I was suddenly dying. I started speaking, but the words froze up in my mind. I spoke anyway, but felt like I rambled incoherently. The glassy camera lens seemed cold and dark. My words tumbled out of me into what felt like a dark, bottomless void. But unfortunately it wasn't a void. At the bottom were long, thin skewers and my mangled words were dinner.

For whatever reasons—perhaps insecurity or teenage angst—the audience I imagined through that camera lens felt hostile. What could have been an absolute blast became agony. I've since conquered my on-camera fears but I never forgot the lesson. We create the audience on the other side of the lens for good or for bad.

The truth is, *all* audiences are imagined to some degree. We imagine what people think of us and then react to that, but we never really know what is inside another person's head. Yet with a live audience there is often some feedback as to what people think or feel regarding our presentation. For example, there might be laughter and applause, or if you're really down on your luck, thrown food of the red and rotten variety.

When you are alone with your video camera there is no feedback. Maybe one day they'll invent video technology that talks back to us like Snow White's magic mirror. But for now video equipment thankfully keeps its opinions to itself and tomatoes remain safely stowed in your fridge. An extended exercise to create what I'm calling your "ideal audience" will follow. For now if you feel nervous, see if you can gently coach yourself out of it. Ask yourself:

*There are very few monsters who warrant the fear we have of them.*

**—Andre Gide**

- ➜ What am I telling myself to cause these feelings?
- ➜ Is there a rational reason to feel this way?
- ➜ Who do I envision speaking to? Is it someone I trust?

### «Try»

How would you rate your comfort level so far? Does it feel natural to speak directly to your camera or is it challenging? If you find it challenging, no reason to worry—there will be plenty of time to relax. Make a note of your tension level so you can compare it to the way you feel at the end of the eight weeks. Choose where you are on a scale from 1 – 10:

1. No difference whatsoever—as if the camera weren't there.

2. More like a heightened awareness and excitement. No anxiety present.

3. Greater feeling of self-awareness, but limited or no anxiety.

4. Not anxious, but feelings of slight awkwardness that come and go.

5. A mixture of anxiety and excitement, but it doesn't keep me from expressing myself.

6. Mild anxiety—heavier on the anxiety than excitement.

7. Moderate anxiety. Feel quite self-conscious but not uncontrollable.

8. Moderate to severe anxiety. Physical symptoms (sweaty palms, elevated heart rate). It's not possible to control the self-conscious feelings.

9. Physical symptoms worsen. Extremely self-conscious.

10. Difficulty speaking coherently. Desire to escape the situation ASAP. Possible panic attacks.

*If you treat every situation as a life and death matter, you'll die a lot of times.*

**—Dean Smith**

Most people will fall somewhere in the range of two to seven. The scores from eight to ten are rare when a person is alone at home with a video camera. However, from my experience working in media (and considering my public access TV debacle), scores from eight to ten are more common when someone is faced with a TV appearance or interview.

If you rated yourself a one, next time you video take a minute to breathe and feel into your body. It's great to be relaxed, but there should also be a certain level of energy present. People who rate themselves as a one may be blocking their physical sensations out of suppressed nervousness.

If you rated yourself somewhere on the higher end, you may find that by gently but firmly sitting yourself back down in front of the camera, the fear response loosens its grip. In the late 1950s psychologist Joseph Wolpe released a study announcing that fears could be decreased by exposure to the same situations that caused them.[2] It's become better known as "desensitization" and numerous studies have since repeated his findings.

If you don't already, one day you will likely view the camera as a trusted (or at least benign) friend rather than a hostile stranger. Following is one further strategy to help get you there. If you feel comfortable on-camera, feel free to skip to the next exercise.

### A Real Turn-off:

*Do you want to know the surefire way to stay anxious? Don't do the thing that makes you nervous!*

**—Larina Kase**

Are you someone who finds that as soon as you hit "record" you freeze up? Or do you have a lingering sense of awkwardness that you can't shake? People who feel this way sometimes learn to hide their anxiety. But slapping a coat of paint over a painful feeling isn't the objective. It doesn't take much for the cracks to show.

Our goal is to feel legitimately comfortable and relaxed on-camera so that: a) you can use the video journal to its fullest potential, and b) you are comfortable when the day arrives that you want or need to present yourself on video publicly.

**«‹Try›»**

- ✦ If you use a video camera with a "flip" style LCD monitor, turn it toward you so you can see your image.
- ✦ If you use a laptop or computer, you should already be able to watch yourself onscreen.

- Start speaking to your camera, *but without hitting record.* This might seem an incongruous exercise, but it can help desensitize yourself to the presence of the camera lens.

- Once you've relaxed, hit "record." Maintain the sense of being in your own private space feeling both calm and comfortable.

Making an unrecorded entry reduces feelings of immediacy and exposure. There is usually less anxiety because of this. This can also be a strategy for divulging something very personal.

Some people wonder how this is any different from speaking alone in a room without a camera. The camera becomes a witness to your words and functions as a focal point. This results in an entirely different experience than if you were alone.

## —Rubber Face—

*You can discover more about a person in an hour of play than in a year of conversation.*

**—Plato**

This goofy but results-rich exercise is borrowed from a popular improvisational theater warm-up. On video, one of the prime ways that we communicate is with our face. But facial expressions are subtle and hard to control. In fact, if we try to control our expressions too much, it backfires. The only real secret is to relax and let go. Creating space for freedom on-camera is also one way of inviting more freedom into life.

### •••Shoot•••

- The idea is this: Become a kid again. Flip on your camera and begin making faces. The loonier the better.

- If you get stuck take a three-part breath, relax and try again.

- Take the exercise a step further and make noises that match the faces. Turn yourself into a living, breathing, howling and hooting cartoon caricature. Be so outlandish that if you were a fly on the wall watching, you'd laugh out loud and wonder if you were crazy (pretend you're a fly of the David Cronenberg variety that can laugh and wonder).

- ✦ What would the owner of a face that looks like the one you're making sound like? Do they have a fast and high-pitched voice, or a slow and laborious one? Are they arrogant, angry, humble or happy?

- ✦ If a particular character arises, name him or her. Maybe they will become a regular cast member on your video journey.

*There was a time when people said, 'Jim, if you keep on making faces, your face will freeze like that.' Now they just say, 'Pay him!'*

**—Jim Carrey**

The people who hate this exercise the most (and I know you're out there) are the ones who can often gain the most from it. Many people who feel self-conscious during this exercise realize that they are "self-monitoring." In other words, they watch their behavior and judge it rather than just relaxing in their own being.

This occurs in life and on-camera. Assumptions are made (that are usually completely wrong) about what people think about us. Meanwhile, an internal critic offers a nitpicking commentary on our behavior like some kind of sadistic sportscaster of life.

Just about anyone over twelve is going to feel critical momentarily when they start acting like a four-year-old on a Guinness-record-breaking sugar high. But realizing that the criticisms and perceived judgments occur alone in a room with an inanimate object can lead to a huge breakthrough. The only person imposing limits on yourself is you.

## —Instant Replay: The Review—

The instant replay is your opportunity to play back what you shot and react to it. It's just as important as the recording. The replay gives you the opportunity to gain perspective. It will be an ongoing component of the *Eight-Week Workshop*.

People often find they look unnatural the first few times. Sometimes this is because they felt tense when they recorded. But most often the criticism is unwarranted and in any case relaxation increases with practice. As you replay your footage, ask yourself:

- ❖ What is your first thought when you see yourself on-camera?
- ❖ Are you being objective? If negative judgments creep in, imagine that you judged a friend the same way. Would this be fair?
- ❖ Pay attention to the particular words you used to express yourself, your mannerisms, and tone of voice. Does the outer you communicate anything about the hidden, inner you?

**"Let go."**

*We live in the world of the instant replay. Around the planet all the events are not only being recorded, but replayed. And ...replay offers a deeper level of awareness than the first play.*

**—Marshall McLuhan**

Learn from your replay, but then move on and make the above two words your motto. There are many things that people say to themselves when they see themselves on-camera, whether for the first time or the fiftieth time. Common negative thoughts and feelings that come up include:

- → I look fat.
- → I look old.
- → I look nervous.
- → I look awkward.
- → I'm boring.
- → I don't look like "myself" at all.

And the list rambles on. But this is where we can observe our judgments with the intent to transform them. Take a pad of paper and write down each thought that comes to mind as you review the footage. Every thought. No matter how trivial. Even if it's just "I feel stupid writing this garbage down." If you notice a thought more than once, write it down again.

The first time I reviewed one of my videos, my blinking and sporadic lip-biting left me cringing, but I forced myself to watch objectively. I didn't love it, but I accepted it. As I become more comfortable, these habits slowly fell away.

The list isn't intended to make you self-conscious, though it may feel that way at first. It's an opportunity to face judgments and work toward acceptance. The judgments are the issue, not the perceived problems. You'll likely also feel pleased with many aspects of your video. Don't forget to include the positive as well.

*The first step toward change is awareness. The second step is acceptance.*
**—Nathaniel Branden**

Keep in mind: Judgments are just thoughts. You can let the negative ones go and affirm the positive. Review your list and cross out the negative judgments. Replace them with either a positive statement or a small, achievable goal that inspires you to improve. For example:

| | |
|---|---|
| ~~"I look nervous."~~ | "Yeah, but I have lots of energy." |
| ~~"I'm not making sense."~~ | "Hey, I'm spontaneous!" |
| ~~"I need to lose weight."~~ | "Okay, I'll get up ten minutes earlier tomorrow and go for a quick walk." |

Everyone judges or criticizes themselves from time to time. But we have a choice. First, we can let the thoughts go and second, we can take action and change things. This is like discovering a cool lake on a scorching summer day. Dipping a toe in feels pleasant, wading in feels wonderful, but it's diving in that changes everything.

Next week you'll have further opportunity to replace criticism with a much more nurturing source: your ideal audience.

*Week Two Notes:*

# Week Two
## Quiet on the Set: Silence the Critic and Create Your Audience

In Fellini's famous movie *8½*, Guido is harassed by Daumier, his harshest and most persistent critic. At one point, Guido fantasizes about hanging Daumier. But Guido no sooner fantasizes this than he chooses to resurrect him and immediately follows his advice anyway.[1]

This happens to us as well. The internal critic appears to look out for our best interests. But he/she/it doesn't. In her book *The New Diary*, Tristine Rainer proposes that the critic creates standards that are impossibly high to achieve. Confronted with these unassailable mountains, we shut down, quit experimenting and, as a result, stop our own growth. Sneaking past the wily critic is one key to full creative expression.

*We are what we think about all day long.*
**—Ralph Waldo Emerson**

Feeling slightly critical is common when starting a new activity. It's especially prevalent in those that involve creativity. People compare themselves or their work (often negatively) with what's already out there. With video in particular there is the yardstick of the highly produced mainstream content we're exposed to daily.

Next you'll ferret out the critic and replace him or her with a much more encouraging source that relies on *internal* rather than external definitions.

### —Looking Outward, Looking Inward—

Most people will have the option of either looking into the camera lens while recording their entry or watching an image of themselves onscreen. If you video your entry on a desktop or laptop computer, this is the default set-up. The software automatically shows what you record. If you use a camcorder, you may or may not be able to easily view yourself, depending on the viewfinder design.

For some, an entry made while watching their image leads to greater self-consciousness. For others, it creates a feeling of greater intimacy;

there is the sense of having a dialog with oneself. This can be powerful especially when talking about emotional issues.

One popular video blogger, Emmalina, interrupts one of her YouTube entries to talk about the pros and cons of watching her image versus looking in the lens. She notices that she looks at her image instead of into the camera and comments that she "hates when people do that." But she proposes that the reason people watch their images while they video is that it feels like they're talking to another human. "When I talk to my webcam it's just a weird plastic thing…When I look at myself it's a bit more normal because it feels like I'm talking to me… and I like talking to me."[2]

Though there's no denying that the camera is, as Emmalina puts it, just a "weird piece of plastic," usually this is quickly forgotten. Looking directly into the lens gives most people the experience of speaking to an audience "out there" even if what they create is private. This is perhaps why it can be challenging.

Nevertheless, both techniques have their place. Also remember that in a live video chat the only way to make "eye contact" with the other person is to look in the *lens*, not at their face onscreen. In the following exercise, you'll experiment with both to experience the difference.

*We are happy when for everything inside us there is a corresponding something outside us.*

**—W.B. Yeats**

**•••Shoot•••**

✦ Watch your onscreen image as you record an entry about the most important thing going on in your life currently.

✦ Speak for at least three minutes—if you run out of specifics, say the first thoughts that come to mind.

✦ What does it feel like to view yourself as you speak? Jot down any impressions that occur.

✦ For your second entry, look directly into the camera lens. Again, describe the most important thing in your life currently. Feel free to add new details as they occur to you.

✦ Note the differences between the two experiences. You may find that the details you include vary considerably between the two techniques.

### ▲Replay▲

❖ Watch both entries. As a *viewer*, how does watching yourself look directly into the lens versus away from it affect you?

❖ Is the method you prefer when watching the same as the one you preferred when shooting?

Some people find that though they prefer not to look in the lens while they record, they miss the sense of contact that looking directly in the lens provides when they review their video later.

*You grow up the day you have your first real laugh—at yourself.*

**—Ethel Barrymore**

## —Quiet the Inner Critic—

The inner critic is a clever adversary. It stifles creativity, compels us to say "no" to opportunities when we might have said "yes," and drains the fun from life. Everyone has internal dialog, but the criticisms often grow even louder in front of a camera. Steven Hayes, psychologist and author of the book *Get Out of Your Mind and Into Your Life*, proposes that seeing our thoughts as reactions (but not who we are) is a key first step to quieting the critic.

### •••Shoot•••

✦ Retell an incident that you've criticized yourself for in the past. For now, give "just the facts," no opinion. Notice when the urge to judge or criticize occurs.

- ✦ Bring this incident to life as much as possible. What were you wearing? What time of year was it? Who were you with? How did you feel? Picture yourself there.

- ✦ Now give voice to any critical thoughts that you have now or that you experienced in the actual situation. Let them flow out of you and disappear into your camera.

### ▲Replay▲

- ❖ Immediately review your entry.

- ❖ As you watch, try to separate the "you" who is watching from the you onscreen while remaining compassionate. Notice if this shifts your perspective.

- ❖ Don't hesitate to talk back to the recording if words to dispute the critic arise.

- ❖ This is the only time you'll ever be specifically asked to do this, but go ahead and ***DELETE the entry.***

- ❖ As you delete the material, imagine the demand for perfection is deleted along with it. Zap! The tyranny of perfection is gone. Well, perhaps not yet, but it's definitely a start.

*Once you accept the fact that you're not perfect, then you develop some confidence.*

**—Rosalynn Carter**

## —Sing It—

Song lights up our brain circuits much differently than speech. Boston University researchers used PET scans to examine which parts of the brain became active when speaking versus singing. The study showed that speech activated the left hemisphere while singing favored the right.[3] The right hemisphere is also the part of our brain that recognizes patterns.

This perhaps explains why many people find it easier to rhyme when they're singing (hip hop anyone?). Added to this, the left brain is known as the critical, analytical side of the brain, while the right brain is known as the artistic, intuitive side. Because singing is very right-brain intensive it's also linked to creativity and problem solving. Perhaps there is truth to working through a problem by "singing the blues away."

**•••Shoot•••**

- ✦ Give a vocal rendition of the three best moments you've experienced today. Waking up and feeling the sun on your face, cuddling with your sweetheart, the first cup of coffee, a warm shower on a cold day are three examples.

- ✦ Weave these moments into a larger song. If the day hasn't been great go with that—belt out a sad song and you may soon forget your troubles.

*A bird doesn't sing because it has an answer, it sings because it has a song.*

**—Maya Angelou**

- ✦ Sing in any style that comes easily: a cheesy musical number, a serenade, a pop ballad, or your own hip-hop tune. Accompany yourself if you play a musical instrument.

- ✦ You'll probably find that it's difficult to take anything too seriously when you sing about it. Singing forces you to breathe, accesses your creative mind, and releases the healing power of vibration.

## —Ban Censorship—

Ideally there is no censorship on "network you" but there often is at first. The censor, that cousin of the critic, likes to make its voice heard whenever something risky or different is attempted. Further, it's not always easy to be completely honest with ourselves. Dr. Ira Progoff, founder of the *Intensive Journal*™ method, once said that the trouble "is that often one lies more to oneself than to anyone else."[4]

Banning censorship doesn't mean that you lay out every secret for the world to view. Yet even people who never plan on showing their video journal publicly may find that they censor.

Have you held yourself back in any of your entries? Following are some common reasons this happens.

### •••Shoot•••

- ✦ Perhaps you fear that someone might view your journal? Make a test entry with your camera on, but don't hit record.

- ✦ Do you watch your image onscreen while you record? Turn this function off for now or keep your eyes focused on the lens so you aren't distracted by your own image.

- ✦ Do you censor certain thoughts? Consider what they might be and if you are ready, take a deep, three-part breath and make an entry about them.

- ✦ If you still feel stuck, use free association to describe where the feeling is located in your body.

*Speak your mind even if your voice shakes.*
**—Maggie Kuhn**

One note, the items we censor may be painful. If the idea of exploring these thoughts is too intense, don't force anything. If certain issues continue to bother you, consider counseling to help work through them.

## ✪ Create Your Ideal Audience ✪

There's always an audience of *some* kind even if you are keeping a video journal rather than a video blog. If you pay attention, you'll notice that you imagine someone (or perhaps a multitude) as you record an entry. This audience might be some aspect of you, God, your higher self or, who knows, maybe your pet dog. This audience occurs with writing as well. On-camera it's intensified. After all, we are being watched, even if only by the camera. The way we feel on-camera is greatly impacted by this audience that is created as an observing presence.

### •••Shoot•••

For this exercise, you'll need your camera, a pen and some paper. Start recording and talk about a defining moment in your life for a minute or two. Ideally something positive. As you speak, check in and try to notice "who" you imagine as your audience.

*My play was a complete success. The audience was a failure.*
**—Ashleigh Brilliant**

- ✦ Imagine that on the other side of the camera lens, almost as if through a window, your audience is watching. Who do you see there? Your boyfriend or girlfriend? Spouse? Father or mother? Indifferent stranger? Worst enemy? Loving crowd of friends?
- ✦ Make a list of every person that came to mind as you spoke.
- ✦ If no specific individuals came to mind, what general sentiment did you receive from your audience?
- ✦ Perhaps you felt there was no audience of any kind. But an empty void is a kind of audience (or lack thereof) and has its own effect. Write it all down.

Now for the second part of this exercise, pick a topic that feels riskier. Consider a difficult circumstance you've faced in the past month. It could be any situation that's been emotionally challenging. For example, a recent conflict with your partner or someone else important in your life, a difficulty at work or some disappointment or sadness. Don't choose something that is so raw and painful you can barely imagine speaking of it. However, it should be something that you'd only discuss with someone close to you.

Describe this situation to your camera taking as long as necessary. Again, jot down who you imagine speaking to as you complete this exercise. For some people, the audience might change from topic to topic.

→ Does the audience shift or stay the same?

→ If the audience shifts, does this affect how you feel?

→ Did speaking about something emotional change the experience?

→ In future exercises, note moments when you feel awkward. Notice times when you feel slightly ridiculous—for example, perhaps during the "Rubber Face" exercise in *Week One*? Who or what flashes through your mind at these times?

*It's the friends you can call up at 4 a.m. that matter.*

**—Marlene Dietrich**

We tend to understand ourselves through our concept of what others think of us.[5] Audiences are often made up of people whose approval is or was important to us. They could be old acquaintances, past colleagues or family members. I was surprised when people I thought (and admittedly wished) I had forgotten about appeared in my audience. If you realize that the person or group of people is not your ideal audience, kick them out of their cushy red velvet seats. Cancel their season tickets and ban them from the sanctuary of your video space.

Who are the people that you trust in your life? Think of at least one person who you could tell anything and they would truly listen. Consider the people who you wouldn't mind being around for those moments when you feel you have made a complete fool of yourself. The folks who would, "love you anyway." If you can't think of specific people, combine the attributes of one or more individuals.

What kind of audience would you trust completely? What kind of audience would you feel love toward? Bring this audience to life in your mind's eye. Imagine their presence.

→ Are they male or female?

→ How old are they?

→ Picture their faces. What do they look like?

→ Hear their voices. What do they sound like?

→ List some of their qualities. Do they have a sense of humor? Are they wise?

*I think that we may safely trust a good deal more than we do.*

**—Henry David Thoreau**

Sometimes the most profound choice is to envision an aspect of yourself. For example, it could be your own higher self or you in the future. The main thing is that your choice resonates with you. Once you've given it some thought, let the thinking go and focus on what felt right. Don't get too caught up in the details—the ideal audience should be a comfortable feeling that you evoke, not something you dwell on.

This ideal audience becomes a safe place you can return to when you're recording. Unseen critics no longer drain your energy. Instead, energy is projected outward into the videos themselves. You'll have a chance to experiment with this further in the next exercise.

## —Meeting Your Audience—

Before hitting record, close your eyes and imagine that your ideal audience sits across from you. Take the time to form a clear image. If you're not the kind of person who thinks in images, recall the feeling that you evoked in the *Ideal Audience* exercise. When you have a clear sense of their presence, start recording.

### •••Shoot•••

- ✦ Greet them. Say their name out loud.
- ✦ Strike up a conversation. Use free association. Ask questions and speak back their imagined answers.
- ✦ If speaking to an imaginary audience makes you feel awkward, tell your audience why you feel this way. Do they respond?

*A true friend is someone who thinks that you are a good egg even though he knows that you are slightly cracked.*
**—Bernard Meltzer**

Having a "dialog" may feel forced and fake at first, but if you push through, it often gets interesting. Keep an open mind. Remember that *whenever* you speak to a camera, you are one way or another talking to an aspect of yourself. Why not embrace this and learn from it? Doing so can help foster a new creative relationship to your inner-self and help you deeply connect with the audience on the other side of the lens.

## —Labels That Limit—

People often define one another by labelling. Labels can be a helpful shorthand that describe roles a person might serve (such as a mother, son, lawyer, secretary, an optimist, pessimist, etc.), but of course the definitions aren't the person.

Labels limit when they go unquestioned. You overlook opportunities because you are <BLANK> (fill in your least favorite label). Most disturbingly, labels sometimes lodge themselves just beneath the surface of awareness, where they do the greatest damage.

### •••Shoot•••

*Don't let the negativity given to you by the world disempower you. Instead give to yourself that which empowers you.*

**—Les Brown**

- ✦ Record every label you can recall being applied to you.
- ✦ What comes to mind as you say each one out loud?
- ✦ What would you say to the people who slapped these labels on you? Do you accept or reject their definitions?
- ✦ There are likely some labels that feel okay to you. Where do these come from? Do they originate from you or from others?
- ✦ Reject labels you no longer want. Experiment with the words. For example, "I no longer accept that I am <BLANK>."
- ✦ Celebrate the labels you accept. For example, "I am proud to be <BLANK>."

Welcome to the end of *Week Two* of your video journey. Next week you'll learn to be present and powerful on-camera. However, there's no need to hurry. Getting past self-criticism is key to everything that follows. If you need to extend a week to repeat exercises or create your own, take as long as you like before continuing.

*Week Three Notes:*

# Week Three

## Be On-Camera: Gain True Camera Presence

The idea of presence on-camera comes from what is called, "stage presence." When he was only sixteen, the famous Welsh actor Richard Burton is said to have stolen the stage during his performance as a lowly extra scrubbing steps. His stage presence was so intense that the audience regularly became distracted from the lead performers even though he had no lines and wasn't a main character. Burton effortlessly stole the show while the leads struggled to win back the spotlight. You can imagine the dirty looks he must have received backstage!

*Paradoxically, it is when we act freely, for the sake of the action itself rather than for ulterior motives, that we learn to become more than what we were.*

**—Mihaly Csíkszentmihályi (from his book *Flow*)**

It's unlikely that Burton intentionally stole the attention. Stage presence came naturally to him. But is it possible to develop? It's generally agreed that stage presence isn't precisely a physical characteristic, but rather an energy that can be sensed by others. People often described Burton's presence as being due to his "stillness." Even when doing "nothing" we constantly emit information that expresses our motivations, thoughts, hopes, and anxieties. You might compare it to a person's aura or energy field—the intensity of the person "being there" in the world.

This also holds true for on-camera presence. The idea is that you need to "be there" fully in front of your camera. The camera is extremely sensitive at picking up presence—whether it is "I feel really nervous" presence or "I am comfortable in my being." Referring to stage presence, people also say that you need to "own it"—to own your space on stage. But how does this apply to you?

Being in the moment (i.e., present) means you aren't thinking about the past or worrying about the future. You are completely engaged. This is true presence. Once achieved it immediately draws others in, both on-camera and off. Luckily, it's not complicated to achieve. It just takes awareness and regular practice.

Perhaps you've heard of the idea of being in "flow" an idea popularized by psychologist Mihaly Csíkszentmihályi? When flow is achieved, people become immersed in their activity and nothing else matters. This state allows them to achieve excellence in performance that they might not otherwise reach. Athletes use this technique and call it "the zone." It's comparable to a kind of active meditation. Everything else seems to disappear because there is laser focus on the necessary task.

Flow isn't something to be forced though. If you try to strong-arm your way into presence, you practically guarantee against it. It is something to be cultivated.

## —Be Present—

Being present is also called being "mindful." Mindfulness is simply being completely aware of what takes place in the present. In short, what we have been talking about. The idea is to quiet the thinking part of the brain. When you think about the past, plan for the future or become *self*-conscious, the moment is yanked away. Yet the present moment is the most powerful place to be in life and on video.

*Observe the space between your thoughts, then observe the observer.*

**—Hamilton Boudreaux**

This is where you might get nervous. How could you possibly function without the past or the future, and would you even want to? Naturally, memories from the past are useful to enjoy and learn from and the future provides goals to plan toward. Being mindful doesn't mean forgetting the past and ignoring the future—it just means that you *choose* where your attention goes.

Mindfulness training such as meditation has been studied at institutions ranging from Harvard to Stanford with compelling results. One study suggests that mindfulness may slow the aging process.[1] Other studies have shown that mindfulness can:[2]

- ➜ Increase relationship satisfaction.
- ➜ Enhance communication ability.
- ➜ Activate the creative mind.
- ➜ Help get a more restful sleep and heal insomnia.

→ Improve mood and reduce stress.

→ Strengthen our ability to adapt to change.

When the present becomes your base, and past and future are tools used by choice, natural presence develops both on-camera and off. You become enigmatic and captivating to whoever your audience may be, and life grows that much easier.

### ✪ Try ✪

Try this exercise without recording for now. If you can, incorporate it into your daily warm-up. It can increase your presence even if done for very short periods. There is a guided version available at www.videoregeneration.com.

*You can learn a lot by watching.*
**—Yogi Berra**

✦ Relax and clear your mind. Take a three-part breath and focus on your body.

✦ Close your eyes. Become aware of your breath traveling in and out of your nose.

✦ How do your feet feel? If you have your shoes off, which part of the heel touches the floor? If you have your shoes on, notice the pressure of the shoe around your foot. Observe as many sensory details as you can.

✦ Return to your breath. Isolate your attention to the sensation of air as it flows past the tips of the nostrils.

✦ Continue this for as long as you like—twenty minutes is ideal. One minute is the minimum and can be very beneficial especially if done several times per day. For longer periods, set your mobile phone alarm. Otherwise, fifteen deep, three-part breaths equal roughly one minute. A full inhale and exhale receives one count.

- When doing this, you will notice *many* thoughts; it's the way our minds work. This is often called "monkey mind." No matter how often you get distracted, when you notice a thought, just say to yourself "thinking" and return to the focus on your breath.

- Counting the breaths helps counter distraction. You can count inhales, exhales or both. Go from one up to ten and then back to one again.

Regularly practice this exercise and you will likely find that your ability to be fully present expands on-camera and off.

**Use Triggers:**

For further benefit, or if you have trouble finding time to do the mindfulness exercise regularly, set up some presence "triggers." The renowned Zen master Thich Nhat Hanh recommends that car drivers not see traffic lights as "an enemy that prevents us from obtaining our goal" but rather a trigger for mindfulness.[3] Other people make a note to become aware of the present moment each time they pass through a door frame or some other aspect of daily life.

*We have more possibilities available in each moment than we realize.*

**—Thich Nhat Hanh**

→ Choose a trigger and when that trigger appears, stop and ask, "What is going on in my mind *now*?" You might be planning, thinking, worrying, etc.; it doesn't matter—no judgments. The point is to develop awareness and observe what is happening in the moment.

→ Choose one trigger for everyday life (for example, red traffic lights) and one for when you video (for example, the red light on your camera, the lens reflection, or a detail on the camera that catches your attention).

Once you become more mindful, you may notice that you start to experience the world slightly differently. You also may find that you gather more material and ideas that you want to record. Usually this isn't just in quantity, but in quality as well. The overlooked details in each moment of life become meaningful.

## —Deep Focus—

With a written journal you can easily stop and look back at prior writing. The moment consists of a series of stops and starts. With video, once we hit "record" we have no choice but to merge into a moving stream of consciousness. We use our minds to pull from the past (by remembering what we've just said) or dive into the future (plan what we'll say next). Yet once each moment passes, it is completely inaccessible until "stop" is pressed on the camera. The following offers the opportunity to maintain presence and focus within this flow of moments and builds on the former exercise.

*The moment one gives close attention to anything, even a blade of grass, it becomes a mysterious, awesome, indescribably magnificent world in itself.*
**—Henry Miller**

### •••Shoot•••

✦ Turn your camera on. Start recording, but sit silently.

✦ Notice your breathing. Feel your stomach rising and falling or the sensation of air as it enters and leaves through your nose.

✦ Focus on the lens with a relaxed gaze and maintain this connection. Be sure to breathe fully and deeply.

✦ If you feel pressure to speak or interact, release that urge. Become comfortable letting the moments flow past you with no pressure to entertain or be anything other than who you are right now. Label any thoughts as "thinking" and let them go.

This exercise encourages awareness of the urge to perform for the camera versus a sense of relaxation and being. This helps connect you with what you truly want to communicate rather than what others think is appropriate. However, sometimes the army brigade of thoughts may seem more like an all-out war for your attention. Don't be discouraged. The simple act of noticing your thoughts and maintaining on-camera stillness even for a few seconds will help you.

- ✦ When you've sat for five or ten minutes (longer if you feel like it), break the silence but maintain your gaze with the camera lens as you begin a video entry.
- ✦ Notice if you developed a stronger connection. To the camera? To yourself? Describe your experience.
- ✦ If you found certain thoughts repeating themselves during your silence, express them.

Videoing after intensive focus tends to be profound because there is much less mental chatter. Additionally, when you focus on the lens and connect, you also strengthen a deep connection with your inner-self.

*Be yourself. The world worships the original.*

**—Ingrid Bergman**

## —Become Powerful On-Camera—

If you try to please others it's tough to be fully present on-camera. Ironically, this doesn't only apply to video blogging. Public or private, the camera is a hugely powerful symbol of the audience. All by itself, it can provoke an urge to perform and knock you out of the moment. You may act like the person you've been told to be rather than who you are inside.

Here's one trick. Decide that the video is for your eyes only. Bill Cosby once said, "I don't know the key to success, but the key to failure is trying to please everybody." Please yourself first. What do you want to say? What is important to you?

Take a deep breath, connect to the present moment and then let it go. Letting go of one moment naturally leads to the next. Feel the energy of your own being. You might feel this as a slight glow in your heart area or possibly a vibrating aliveness in your body. When you tap into this, expression happens naturally. You share your true self.

When faced with a "live" situation where you participate in a video chat or interview, the above still applies. Remain in the present and listen to the other participants. Too often we think of the future (what we are going to say) or the past (what we should or should not have said) and end up clueless as to what's going on right now. Video is a high-speed medium, and if you don't stay grounded in the moment, you'll be left behind.

## •••Shoot•••

What are some characteristics you'd like to express more fully? This can be either in life or on-camera. Expression on-camera gives you practice in finding your voice in life. For this exercise, imagine that you speak to a large audience, perhaps in the thousands or even millions.

*To avoid criticism, do nothing, say nothing, and be nothing.*
**—Elbert Hubbard**

- ✦ Introduce yourself to this audience.
- ✦ Without forcing it, express several qualities that you honestly appreciate in yourself. You don't need to make it all-inclusive.
- ✦ What three things matter to you most in life? What would you fight for (or against)?
- ✦ Now tell this audience some of the qualities that you know could use some work. No self-bashing, just a couple of areas that you're striving to improve.
- ✦ Pay attention to the thoughts behind your words. Notice if negative judgments creep in, but don't do anything about them. Just let them go.

Nelson Mandela quoted Marianne Williamson in one of his speeches when he said that, "our deepest fear is not that we are inadequate, but that we are powerful beyond measure." You've probably heard this before. Thinking about the entry you just recorded, does it resonate with you?

If this exercise challenged you, try it again with Mandela's voice in mind. What would it feel like to be able to speak to an audience of any size and maintain your presence? You can tap into an internal source of strength by listening to your inner compass and remaining present.

For some, this exercise comes easily—perhaps too easily. But when people are overly proud of themselves and their achievements, in other words arrogant, it may mean they don't feel one hundred percent comfortable with themselves. If this might describe you, try the exercise again. Pay attention to where the need to impress comes from. Can you just be yourself or do you need to be something "larger?" Allow yourself to stand in front of an audience that you don't need to impress. Where you are enough just the way you are.

*Where there is anger, there is always pain underneath.*

**—Eckhart Tolle**

## —Transform Anger—

Anger kills. This is according to anger expert Dr. Redford Williams at the Duke University Medical Center. Because of this, Williams considers anger management as crucial to health as diet and exercise.[4] In general, unexpressed anger is a poison that inflicts immense damage. Chronic anger can show up as tension in the neck, back and shoulders. After a while this becomes habitual, and the emotional and physical body shuts down and becomes constricted.

Recall someone you still hold anger toward. Imagine them in front of you. Now you can express yourself truthfully. Give yourself permission to feel anger without guilt or judgment. If you shout, that's fine, but no need to force anything. Though it can be beneficial with proper guidance, one study found that intentionally "venting" by hitting pillows and screaming increased rather than reduced anger.[5]

### •••Shoot•••

- ✦ Tell this individual why you are (or were) angry. Fully express yourself without forcing it.
- ✦ Notice where the anger lives in your body.
- ✦ Can you separate yourself from the feelings?
- ✦ Emotions are compared to "waves" for a reason. They ebb and flow and sometimes just when we think we've leapt above the biggest one, an even larger one crashes in. There is no hurry.
- ✦ When you've expressed yourself fully, think of one positive quality about this person and share it. If this becomes excruciatingly difficult, perhaps try the exercise again!

*You can't stop the waves, but you can learn to surf.*

**—Jon Kabat-Zinn**

### ▲Replay▲

- ❖ Either immediately afterward or sometime during the week, review the above exercise. Anger is one of the most difficult emotions to face and the review can be challenging.
- ❖ But anger is simply energy and it's nothing to be ashamed of. Be proud for having the guts to express it. Remember that the energy of anger can be redirected and transformed.
- ❖ Take a deep breath and ground yourself in the present moment. Realize that the you who watches the video, and the angry person on-screen, are separate.
- ❖ If you still feel anger, try to notice the sensation in your body and observe it as energy rather than attaching the label "anger" to it.

When we watch our anger rather than becoming engulfed by it, anger can be acted *from* rather than acted *on*. Witnessing anger opens up the possibility of incorporating the energy behind it without the negative charge. When this is done in life, the passion can be used to create the changes we crave rather than blowing up and causing destruction.

## —Shhh...—

Whispered words take on a completely new meaning. Whenever whispering happens around us, it immediately catches our attention. Performers make use of this onstage—dramatically lowering their voices to force us to pay close attention to the words they speak.

Making a whispered entry can be an emotional and moving experience. You'll want to be closer to your camera to make sure your whisper is heard.

*A whisper can be stronger, as an atom is stronger, than a whole mountain.*

**—Louise Nevelson**

### •••Shoot•••

✦ Confide a time you felt vulnerable. Does whispering make it easier? What emotions arise?

✦ Whisper several things you appreciate about yourself or someone you love. Notice the quality of tenderness that whispering evokes.

✦ Whisper something that you would normally want to shout. Experience how it feels to whisper when you want to yell.

### ▲Replay▲

❖ How does watching this entry affect you?

❖ Do you find that the importance of your words is enhanced or diminished?

- Whispering often reveals vulnerability. As you view this whispered entry try to foster a sense of love and compassion for the person on-screen.

## —Loving Them Bones—

When you consider your physical body, what comes to mind? Do you feel satisfied or dissatisfied looking in the mirror? How about on-camera?

Feeling comfortable with your physical self is important. The physical body is the prime instrument of communication: not just your mouth, not even just your face—your entire body. The way you sit, the way you breathe, the way you move—these form an integrated impression of who you are out in the world. This is perceived on a subtle level by others during everyday interactions. It becomes magnified on video.

*Even, today, when people tell me I'm beautiful, I do not believe a word of it.*

**—Uma Thurman**

When you think about people who have charisma on-camera, it's not necessarily about stereotypical definitions of attractiveness. Online video breaks some of the physical stereotypes set by Hollywood. Not everyone has perfect teeth; not everyone is model attractive. For example, consider Gary Brolsma of *Numa Numa* fame. Millions enjoyed his video. Though Brolsma isn't conventionally attractive, he is comfortable in his being and, as a result, charismatic.

In this exercise, wear as little or as much clothing as you feel comfortable with. This could mean underwear, your bathing suit, shorts and a T-shirt, or even naked.

### •••Shoot•••

- Once you are ready—start recording. If you have a camera where you can flip the viewfinder around to see what you're shooting, do that. If you're recording yourself on your computer, you should already be able to see yourself on the screen. Otherwise, have a mirror nearby so that you can use your reflection as your reference (but this is second best).

- What initial impressions occur when you see your image on screen?

- Are your eyes drawn to one part of your body more than another? If so why?

- Describe what you see. Keep in mind that it's not an urban legend: viewing yourself on video does add some weight. This happens because a moving three-dimensional object is being represented in two dimensions.

- Does your video self accurately capture the "real" you? How does the experience differ from looking in a mirror?

- Many of us have issues with the way our bodies look on some level. The media presents such unobtainable standards that it's challenging not to. The more you can let these go, the more comfortable you'll be on-camera and in life.

- Remember that your video image is an illusion made of tiny pixels of energy. In a similar way, quantum physics has shown your physical body to be an illusion made from atomic particles of energy.

- Gently place one hand in the center of your chest. Visualize as many parts of your body as you can at one time: from the hair on your head to the nails on your toes. Send a burst of love and appreciation to every particle of your being.

*You don't have a soul. You are a Soul. You have a body.*

**—C.S. Lewis**

Finally, if you chose to do this exercise with little clothing—or even naked—ensure that this recording *remains private.* I can't stress this enough. To place a vivid image in your mind, this is *not* the video that you want to accidentally attach as your video résumé one sleepy morning.

You might even consider doing this exercise without hitting the record button if you're concerned. You'll still benefit. Or delete it directly after reviewing. Though you'll miss out on the opportunity to look back at your video in ten years (and wonder what you ever complained about), the peace of mind may be worth it.

Next week, you'll continue to build on your work thus far as you integrate video with the everyday in order to live life "cinematically."

*Week Four Notes:*

# Week Four
## Shoot From the Heart: Living Cinematically

Video blogger Will Luers proposes that when people poke fun at the homegrown production and entertainment values of video blogs, they overlook an important aspect. In the video blogging experience, it's about making one's life "cinematic."[1]

Living life cinematically offers the opportunity to view every moment of life as a significant moment. This doesn't mean that each second needs to be recorded—your friends and family would avoid you like the flu—and in fact that type of obsessive intensity is the opposite of what I'm talking about. Realizing that "worthy" moments occur all the time encourages a shift in thinking.

You are the star in your own life movie. This has nothing to do with ego, the number of online viewers, or even having viewers at all. Each moment, even the seemingly dull, can be rife with meaning if you pay attention. Boldly and specifically capturing significant moments lets you define life creatively by your own standards. In other words, shooting from the heart rather than the head.

*The camera is an instrument that teaches people how to see without a camera.*

**—Dorthea Lange**

### —The Little Things in Life—

It's easy to overlook the small details that make up a life. Yet the small details can help us see the larger picture. Spend a day (or you could make it the entire week) where you slow down, open your senses and pay attention. Keep everything that passes through your hands during the period. For example, the ephemera of life: receipts, pay stubs, tickets, flyers, and so forth.

**•••Shoot•••**

At the end of the period, show each item to your camera and explain the details surrounding them.

- ✦ Who was present when you bought your subway or bus fare or paid for parking?
- ✦ What were the sights, sounds and smells at that moment?
- ✦ What was the employee wearing who gave you the receipt for your morning coffee?
- ✦ Did you take a flyer from a person on the street? What did the person look like? Describe the street at that moment in time.
- ✦ Bring these remembered moments to life with words, voice, face, and body.

*A lot of people don't realize what's really going on. They view life as a bunch of unconnected incidents 'n things. They don't realize that there's this, like, lattice of coincidence that lays on top o' everything.*

***—Repo Man***

Pay attention to synchronicities that occur as you work through this exercise. Carl Jung defines synchronicities as "acausal connectors." They are meaningful coincidences that occur throughout life. We can learn from synchronicity, and they help keep us on track, but we often miss them completely in our distracted, multi-tasked lives.

## —Create Change—

Beginning to pay attention to synchronicity can lead to the realization that change is needed. It's easy to get caught up in the day-to-day details of life and overlook the themes that interweave themselves.

People often make resolutions to create change, especially on New Year's Eve. But resolutions are one of the biggest scams going—they usually don't have staying power. You focus on what you want but often end up getting what you don't want. Instead, why not focus on what you already have first? By focusing on the positive themes (what you're grateful for), the negative is crowded out.

Along these lines, a recent study at George Mason University found that feeling grateful was "one of the strongest contributors to well-being."

Gratitude increased psychological and physical health at the same time it decreased depression and anxiety.[2]

### •••Shoot•••

- ✦ During this week, record five things each day that you feel grateful for and one thing that you'd like to change.
- ✦ It's easy to describe the people, places, things, that we feel gratitude for but don't forget to record the "why"—the reason for your gratitude.
- ✦ Every day, make sure that your entry includes *different* items. You'll very likely feel grateful for the same thing more than once during the week. Resist the urge to fall back on what's comfortable. The things that don't come to mind as easily are sometimes the most valuable.
- ✦ You might discover that things you felt needed changing aren't a problem at all, but it is only your thinking "that has made them so." Sometimes thoughts need changing, not the situation. This exercise will help make the difference apparent.

*It's not about how to achieve your dreams. It's about how to lead your life. If you lead your life the right way, the karma will take care of itself. The dreams will come to you.*

**—Randy Pausch**

The idea is to expand the number of things for which you feel grateful. If you have trouble thinking of things at the beginning of the exercise, you likely won't by the end.

## —Dream Out Loud—

Numerous books on journaling encourage writing down goals to help focus and commit to your aspirations. With video journaling you get to speak, sing, or shout your goals and dreams out loud. Later, the goals are further reinforced when you review your entries and hear your own words. Immediate feedback is given and received.

What would you like to create in your life? Everyone has goals unique to their personality and life circumstance. Most people have dreams they've neglected. Speaking goals aloud puts creative energy behind them and opens the door for taking concrete action to manifest them.

For this exercise, remember to speak with intent. For example, if your dream is to finish your college degree, the intent may be to live your life fully. Intent is the spark that ignited you, the raw fuel that propels you toward the goal: your larger purpose. Being clear on your intent leaves open the possibility that goals might be fulfilled in ways that haven't occurred to you.

### •••Shoot•••

- ✦ State one life goal that you're working toward. Why is this achievement important to you?
- ✦ Describe one material item you'd like to own. What made you choose this one over others?
- ✦ Communicate one state of being you'd like to experience in your life more often. For example, peace, clarity, or creativity.
- ✦ State your goals as if they were present achievements. How does it feel to have the camera record this moment?

*Dream as if you'll live forever, live as if you'll die today.*

**—James Dean**

### ▲Replay▲

- ❖ What thoughts occur as you hear your goals and aspirations spoken back to you?
- ❖ Do you believe that you truly desire your goals? Why or why not?
- ❖ If you find that you question your commitment, remind yourself that you have the right to your aspirations.

- Record a new version if you feel the need.

## —Story Power—

In the legend of the *1,001 Nights*, it is "story power" that saves a young Princess's life. When the King's wife is unfaithful, he declares *all* women unfaithful and has his advisor supply virgins that he marries in the evening and has executed by morning. Seeing the terrible injustice in the King's agenda, Scheherazade, the advisor's virgin daughter, bravely volunteers. Her father is terrified for her life. What he doesn't realize is that his daughter has a plan.

That evening, Scheherazade tells the King a story so rich in detail that he nearly forgets where he is. Dawn breaks and he hurries her to finish it so he can execute her, but she protests that there is not enough time. Her life is spared and she continues her incredible stories the next night, and then the next. For the following one thousand and one nights, she saves her life by telling stories. During this time, the King falls in love with her, changes his evil ways, and ultimately spares her life making her the Queen.

*There is no greater agony than bearing an untold story inside you.*
**—Maya Angelou**

Your situation is hopefully not as high stakes as Scheherazade's, but daily life is made up of stories both short and long. Telling your colleague what you did over the weekend is a story. Explaining a movie you saw or a cause you're involved with to a friend are also stories. Even outlining why you deserve a raise can be a story. If your storytelling skills are strong, you engage and influence your listeners. If your storytelling skills are weak, friends and family listen because they love you, others tune out (and you may not get that raise).

The so-called life of the party is often the person who can captivate a group of people with something that happened to him or her. It's often not what they're saying, it's the detail and style with which they say it. Experiences spring to life fed by descriptions that form vibrant, mental pictures. That's one of the keys to strong storytelling—describing things with such passion that they become real for others.

In any story, the words your listeners hear carry a small fraction of the total meaning—about fifteen percent.[3] The remaining eighty-five percent comes from your gestures, facial expressions, timing, intonation, eye contact, and general engagement.

As Annette Simmons tells it in her book, *The Story Factor*, in many ways "you are a story to everyone you meet." In the video realm, this is even more the case. Telling your stories on-camera will enhance your storytelling skills while you build up an archive of life's most significant moments.

### •••Shoot•••

- ✦ Recall a primary event from your life, ideally a moment that changed you, and record the story from beginning to end.
- ✦ Add details—think sound, sight, touch, taste, and smell. What was it like to be there? Bring yourself back to that point in time.
- ✦ Be specific. Your story will become immensely more interesting as a result. By being specific you ironically make your story more universal.
- ✦ If it makes sense, provide some dialog. What were people saying? You don't need to be an actor to pretend to be someone else. Have fun with it. Modify your voice and body language to match thcirs.
- ✦ Feel free to record this a few times until you feel satisfied.

*To be a person is to have a story to tell.*

**—Isak Dinesen**

### ▲Replay▲

When you review, watch for:

- ❖ Does your story have a beginning, middle, and an end? Not every story follows this pattern, but many do. If yours doesn't, make sure it's a choice.

- Did you start to ramble? When we tell personal stories it's easy to become sidetracked. Try setting a strict two-minute time limit then tell your story again.

- Is there life and vibrancy in your words? If not, go back and give it another go. Tell the story as if a group of excited school children were clustered around you. There is no need to be patronizing or gushing, but give it some spark and energy.

- Watch your video without sound. Notice the gestures and facial expressions that you used, without judging them.

- If you seem inauthentic or lack expressiveness, record it again. Consider what makes this story important to you. Connect to your passion and excitement and your natural gestures and expression will follow.

*If you've heard this story before, don't stop me, because I'd like to hear it again.*

**—Groucho Marx**

### •••Shoot•••

- Imagine that someone has just asked you "What's your story?" Respond to them.

- Tell "your story," taking as long as you need to.

- Have any archetypes woven themselves through your life? For example, the child (innocent, lighthearted), the hero (strong sense of mission, tenacity in the face of adversity), the victim (often feels taken advantage of, powerless), the mother (nurturing, takes care of others—can be male or female), the trickster (a renegade who flouts the traditional).

- Include archetypes that resonate with you, but don't be bound to them. They are included to get you thinking.

### ▲Replay▲

- ❖ Storytelling taps into the unconscious mind, especially when life stories are told. Did any surprising thoughts or images occur as you watched yourself?
- ❖ Note your reactions. Did you leave out anything important? Is there something you would like to highlight?
- ❖ You will never be able to include every detail, but see if you communicated the *essence* of who you are. Figuring out what that is can be as beneficial as telling the story itself.
- ❖ Continue to record stories as they occur to you throughout the week and beyond. Storytelling is one of the core video journaling activities that can enhance and maintain creativity.

*We like our archetypes and heroes to be what they are at face value. And life doesn't work out like that.*

**—Laura Dern**

## —Video Self-Portrait—

A video self-portrait offers the opportunity to carve your own path toward a cinematic life. Similar to a painted or photographic self-portrait, the idea is to capture an aspect of your inner-self. This doesn't have to be all-encompassing or defining. It could just be what you're feeling today. The important thing is to follow your gut reaction.

For this first self-portrait the task is kept simple with several imposed constrictions. These might seem limiting at first, but many people find that paring down their basic options paradoxically enhances creativity.

### •••Shoot•••

- ✦ Keep the camera stationary. You can start and stop your camera, but otherwise, no editing.

- Create a self-portrait without using words or speech. It should be no more than five minutes in length.

- Use gestures, facial expression, pantomime, physical actions, sound, art, sketches, photographs, written words, changes of clothes or even costume, and whatever else you might think of. Or include nothing but you.

- Allow your imagination (and unconscious mind) free rein!

### ▲Replay▲

- What aspect of yourself did you capture?

- If this is an aspect of yourself you'd like to enhance, consider how you might do that.

*Don't think. Thinking is the enemy of creativity.*
**—Ray Bradbury**

You'll have the chance to make a second video portrait with expanded objectives during *Week Eight.*

## ✪ Alternate Replay Method ✪

Up until now, you've reviewed your entries and made notes on paper as needed. The following replay method is slightly more complicated but offers a new level of interaction. You watch and react to your own video while you record. For example, if you recorded your video using a camcorder, you would watch the footage on your computer while you record your reaction, comments, etc., to what you view.

This method won't work for everyone and depends on how comfortable you are with your equipment. For those who can, it is quick and fun. Once you're set up you can respond in the moment to what you see without worrying about writing it down.

Then when you have time, you can also review the commentary video if you like. This gives you the opportunity to view the effect that watching your video has on you. It's worth doing it at least once for this reason alone.

- ✦ Pay attention to when you appear tense or when you relax. What seems to make you tense up? What seems to make you comfortable?

- ✦ If you're feeling ambitious, you might even edit the commentary and your original video together and juxtapose them if you've made helpful observations.

Subsequent exercises will include various replay sections. You can either try these the first way (using a pen and paper to record your thoughts and make notes) or use the above alternate method. Remember that the ✪ symbol means there is a video explanation available at www.videoregeneration.com.

*We continue to shape our personality all our life. If we knew ourselves perfectly, we should die.*

**—Albert Camus**

Congratulations! This brings us to the halfway mark. Now is a great point to pause and take stock of how you're doing. If you like, revisit some of the earlier exercises to see how your experience of video is evolving. Up next you'll learn to have fun with framing and find out why camera angles can have attitude.

*Week Five Notes:*

# Week Five
## Production Design: Angles Are Attitudes

Through both practice and training, people who make their living in front of the lens learn to present themselves on-camera. Watch a newscast or hosted show from any major network. Notice how seldom the hosts touch their chins, bite their lips, scratch their noses, or rock back and forth. When it does happen, it's often for comedic effect. Professionals on-camera tend to make small, rather controlled gestures because every movement looks larger on TV than it really is.

Watch video blogs and, refreshingly, you will find all of the above norms broken over and over again. But before you know it—even the rule-breaking becomes an unspoken convention. Several YouTube videos poke fun at the clichés that have risen around online video such as quick cuts and shaky handheld footage. This week you'll have the chance to experiment with *your* personal on-camera style.

*To be normal is the ideal aim of the unsuccessful.*

**—Carl Jung**

### —On-Camera Style—

Perhaps you don't plan on video blogging. Why should you care about on-camera style? For two reasons: First, the more authentic your presence, the more you gain when you look back at your entries. Even people recording private journals may find that the style of the videos they have watched on TV or online influences them more than they realized. Second, as mentioned earlier, even if you don't make your video journal public, in an increasingly video-oriented world you may sooner rather than later find yourself in front of a camera.

**«Try»**

- ✦ Pay attention during your next video entry, notice what conventions you might unconsciously follow.

- Do you speak a certain way or stick to certain topics? What about your personal style and the way you move? No judgments, just be aware as to what you chose and why.

Aesthetic norms are good to have in your toolbox but creativity killers if they're taken as law. There are no precise ways of saying when you should break or follow rules—that would just be another kind of rule! In the end, the best advice is to be familiar with the norm but follow your instincts.

## —On-Camera Movement—

There is no correct or incorrect way to move on-camera. What might be irritating and distracting coming from one person could seem authentic and engaging from another. It also depends on the purpose of your video. Shooting a video for a job interview will have a very different goal than a journal entry to vent frustration. Next you'll explore three different ways of moving on-camera so you can learn what effect each has on you.

*The merit of originality is not novelty; it is sincerity.*

**—Thomas Carlyle**

### •••Shoot•••

- Make a one-minute entry describing the most unique experience that occurred in the past month. It doesn't need to be dramatic, but should be meaningful to you. Intentionally use plenty of broad, sweeping hand gestures and body movements. Move toward and away from the camera frequently.

- Make a second brief entry on this same experience. Make expressive gestures, and move as much as you like, but keep within the boundaries of the frame, in other words, what your camera can see.

- ✦ Make a third entry where you don't move at all. Allow yourself to make facial expressions, but otherwise keep your body frozen.

**▲Replay▲**

- ❖ How does each video entry affect you? Were your topics influenced by your movements?

- ❖ What impression might you have of someone who moved as often or as seldom as you just did? Notice what felt natural.

## —Connecting to Your Audience—

*By the way: thank you. Without you I'd just be a weirdo, talking to myself.*

**—Ze Frank**

Your eyes are the strongest connection to your audience, whether that audience is you, a family member, or hundreds of thousands of people. The only way to reach the viewers on the other side of the lens is through it.

Studies show that video distance learning among students increases when teachers make direct eye contact with the camera lens.[1] It can take courage to make a strong connection to a camera lens, but when you are able to, the effect is profound.

Some believe that each blink is one less connection that you form with your viewers. Ze Frank, an early video blogger, made a point of *never* blinking. He developed a cult following for about a year with his *The Show With Ze Frank.* Episodes are still available for viewing online if you want to check them out. Never blinking takes it to a bit of an extreme, though it worked for him. He draws you in immediately and you don't want to stop watching or dare blink yourself.

Frequent blinking may diminish the connection; but how far you take this to is up to you. Steadily looking into the lens without a break could come across as engagement...or as glaring, and that may not be your goal. In *Week One*, you experimented with the effect of watching your own image versus looking into the camera lens while you recorded. The following exercise gives you the chance to explore this from a different perspective.

### •••Shoot•••

- ✦ Make a one-minute entry *never* looking into the lens or anywhere near it. Instead look into the space around and above the camera. Notice how this feels.
- ✦ Make a one-minute entry where your eye contact varies: sometimes looking in the lens, and other times above, below or to the sides.
- ✦ Make a one-minute entry where you look directly into the camera lens without taking your eyes off it for even an instant. Experiment with how much you blink—from frequently to barely at all.

Remain present and in the moment. Engage with what you're communicating, and imagine it flowing out through your eyes to the audience. If you have trouble, revisit the *Ideal Audience* exercise in *Week Two.*

*The countenance is the portrait of the soul, and the eyes mark its intentions.*

**—Cicero**

### ▲Replay▲

- ❖ Notice how much eye contact felt natural to you as the viewer.
- ❖ Throughout the week, pay attention to the amount of eye contact you make with people in everyday conversation. How does this compare to your experience on-camera?

## ✪ Your Authentic Voice ✪

Voice is a sometimes overlooked but crucial element of self-expression and emotional engagement. It is one of the main elements we subconsciously pay attention to when experiencing someone's presence on-camera or off. Voice is more than just words and sound. Ideally rising from the belly (the diaphragm), your authentic voice is an auditory fingerprint of your being.

Some people believe that developing their voice means changing its sound. For example, many people, especially men, deepen the voice to make it sound richer. This almost always comes across as fake; so unless you're doing it for comic effect, best to skip it. What is helpful is to learn how to connect to your vocal instrument.

When people discuss singing, you'll often hear them mention the diaphragm. The diaphragm is a group of muscles attached to the bottom of your ribs, sternum and upper lumbar region. It has the rather handy function of keeping you alive by allowing you to breathe. By moving downward (pulling air in) and upward (pushing air out), oxygen is inhaled and exhaled.

When you speak, the diaphragm regulates the rate at which air flows past the vocal chords. Its movement creates a cushion of air that allows your voice to resonate. The following will help you get a better sense of the way your diaphragm works.

*Let your voice and being flow with the Tao.*

**—Stephen Chun-Tao Cheng**

✦ Find a chair that has adequate back support and sit up straight. Now let out a long "ah" sound in whatever way feels natural to you.

✦ Keep the sound going for as long as you can.

Many people use their chest to initiate the sound. They keep using their chests until their diaphragms naturally take over right when they're about to run out of breath. The goal is to develop awareness of the diaphragm so that, whether singing or speaking, we provide air pressure with our diaphragm, not our chests.

✦ Let out an "ah" sound again. This time let your stomach push out just a bit.

✦ Place your hands on your lower abdomen and apply some gentle pressure.

- As you let out an "ah," visualize the sound coming up from your belly, and gently press this area. Don't push your stomach muscles though—the area should be firm, but relaxed. You may notice that the sound becomes naturally more resonant when you try this.

The same principle applies to speaking. Sit up straight and place your hand on your belly to bring your awareness there. Say a few words. It may take several tries, but you should start to notice a difference. Keep practicing as you make your entries and your vocal tone and resonance will continue to move toward their full potential.

Another way to expand vocal tone is to allow resonance to occur in your mouth and chest cavity rather than your nose (which causes a thinner, nasal quality). Plug your nose with two fingers and say your favorite cartoon character several times. If you feel vibration in your fingers, you're using nasal resonance. Place one hand on your sternum and try again. Visualization is key when it comes to voice—imagine sound filling your torso. You should feel increased vibration in your chest and less at your nose. Your voice becomes naturally more resonant without changing its pitch.

*The physical world, including our bodies, is a response of the observer. We create our bodies as we create the experience of our world.*

**—Deepak Chopra**

### •••Shoot•••

- Take shallow breaths and allow your chest to collapse. Free-associate for one minute on whatever thoughts naturally arise.

- Sit up straight and allow your belly to support your diaphragm. Place your hand there as a gentle guide. Again, free-associate.

- It may seem obvious (and this exercise takes it to an extreme), but posture affects your voice, which in turn affects your state of being and energy level.

- Was there a difference between the two in terms of what you free-associated *about*? The observing mind has a profound connection to the physical body.

## —Fun with Framing—

Orson Welles used low angles throughout most of *Citizen Kane.* In the first part of the movie, Kane is brash and wields his power effortlessly. Shot from low angles in small rooms and claustrophobic spaces, he is dominant and imposing. By the end of the film, Kane has lost his influence. He is still shot from a low angle, but the vastness of Xanadu towers over him and he seems diminished.

In *Blade Runner*, there are many high angle shots. *Blade Runner* borrows heavily from the "film noir"—a genre that used this aesthetic frequently. In *Blade Runner,* the high angles give a sense of fatality and of humans being crushed by technology and their circumstances.

Anyone with a favorite film director knows that entire careers are built from judicious placement of camera for aesthetic impact. From my own experience in production, camera placement also changes the emotional tone of the location. Try the suggestions below and see how each camera set-up changes not only the aesthetics of your video, but the emotional experience of the moment.

*Create your own visual style... let it be unique for yourself and yet identifiable for others.*

**—Orson Welles**

### Distance:

We already experimented with camera distance during the first week. Here's your chance to take that even further.

#### •••Shoot•••

- ✦ Start an entry from as far away as you can move from your camera—in other words, an extremely "wide angle" shot. Free-associate and describe how it feels to be standing such a long distance away from the camera. You may need to shout!
- ✦ Continue speaking as you slowly walk closer.
- ✦ Notice the points where you feel a "shift." The best way to describe this is to think of personal space. You've probably had

the experience where someone, just by moving a few inches toward you, suddenly "invaded" your personal space. It's as if an invisible boundary were crossed. That's what you're looking for.

- Each time that you feel a shift in your body, stop and describe the difference. It might be an emotion or memory that arises or the urge to adjust your posture. Don't forget to breathe.

- Continue moving in increments, stopping when you feel the need, until you are within an inch of touching the camera lens—an "extreme close-up," to say the least. You'll likely be out of focus, but that's okay. What is the most surprising thought or feeling that occurs to you when you get this ultra-close to the camera?

- We all have various unseen boundaries surrounding our bodies that vary with the circumstances. This exercise not only gives you the chance to experiment with the aesthetics of different distances, but also gives you the opportunity to fine-tune your body awareness in relation to your camera.

*There is only you and your camera. The limitations in your photography are in yourself, for what we see is what we are.*

**—Ernst Haas**

**Framing:**

Framing refers to your position in relation to the boundaries of the screen. The amount of space to the left or right of your body and above your head has an aesthetic and emotional impact. If you "cut off" part of your body, especially part of your face, this also has an interesting effect.

**•••Shoot•••**

We all deserve to be treated with respect and if certain lines are crossed, we need to assert ourselves. Yet sometimes we create boundaries in the form of self-imposed limitations and believe they are real.

In this exercise, you'll explore some of the boundaries in your life. Where have you been either held back or helped by boundaries? Which did you create, and which came from others?

- Set up a shot with maximum headroom. Headroom is the space above your head in the frame. Frame the shot so that your chin is touching the bottom of the lower frame. Speak about a time when you felt limitless freedom to do whatever you wanted.

- Position yourself at the far right of the frame. Roughly half of your face should be off-screen. Recall a time when people in your life created boundaries that excluded you or didn't take your needs into consideration.

- Now set up a shot with your head perfectly centered in the frame. Identify the boundaries that you have placed around yourself. These are often the hardest ones to notice.

- Try other framings of your own invention or that you've seen online or in movies.

*A style is not a matter of camera angles or fancy footwork, it's an expression, an accurate expression of your particular opinion.*

**—Karel Reisz**

### ▲Replay▲

- Which framings do you like more than others? Aesthetically? Emotionally?

- Is there a valid reason that framing on most TV shows and many video blogs tends to fall into a few repeated patterns?

- Did the framing affect the perception you had of yourself? Did it change the impact of what you said by either enhancing or diminishing your expression?

## ✪ Angles Are Attitudes ✪

Up until now, the angle you've likely shot most of your video from is eye-level. The eye-level angle is comfortable. It conveys a certain equality and sense of easy engagement with the camera.

It might seem obvious, but wherever you place your camera is where you place your audience. In other words, camera placement determines the perspective they will view you from. Keep that in mind as you experiment with the following.

### High Angle:

In a high angle, the camera is above and you look up at it from below. Either place the camera above you, or get down low beneath the lens.

If you use a fixed camera such as a built-in laptop camera, you'll need to get creative. Place a cushion on the floor. Sit down and look up toward your camera. For other types of cameras, miniature tripods aren't expensive and greatly increase your range of possibilities.

*Genius is childhood recaptured.*
**—Jean Baudrillard**

Looking up at the camera can endow it with a paternal element or create the feeling of speaking up to God or a higher authority. From the audience's perspective, the person being videoed may seem less powerful. Note, though, that whatever angle you choose, these are just possible perceptions. We can create from a place of power wherever we stand whether on-camera or in life.

**•••Shoot•••**

- ✦ **Child's POV:** Speak from the point of view of you as a child. Pick a specific age. Recall a childhood experience that you'd like to preserve for posterity or that still holds an emotional charge. If you're feeling gutsy, speak as if you really were that child at that age.

- ✦ **Equals:** Recall someone who intimidated you in the past. Speak to them as an equal. Explain why you no longer feel intimidated.

Remind yourself that no matter what the outward appearance, we are fundamentally equal.

**Low Angle:**

In a low angle, you look down at your camera lens from above. Standing up and looking down at your camera works just fine. You can even experiment with putting the camera on the floor for an extreme effect.

From the viewer's perspective this is the "hero's shot." The person may be viewed with a sense of reverence. In this position, there is often a perceived feeling of strength and power.

**•••Shoot•••**

*Cock your hat—angles are attitudes.*
**—Frank Sinatra**

✦ Tap into your pride. Talk about one of your proudest moments. Does the camera angle accentuate your feelings?

✦ Tap into your strength. Speak about a cause that is important, someone you admire, or a time in your life when you demonstrated strength in the face of adversity.

✦ Relive your happiest moment. Describe it as if it were happening right now. Relive the wonderful feelings you had, and express them using your entire body.

✦ Consider trying the above looking up at the camera instead of down at it (high angle instead of low angle). See if this changes your experience.

**"Dutch" or "Batman" Angle:**

In the 1930s and 1940s, German directors experimented with shooting scenes at an angle to create uneasiness in their audiences. One of the earliest films to use this technique was the expressionistic classic *The Cabinet of Dr. Caligari* directed by Robert Wiene.

The word *Deutsch* (i.e., German) was sometimes confused with the word "Dutch," hence the name. In more recent times, it came to be known as the "Batman" angle for more obvious reasons. Experiment with your own versions of Dutch angles from a minimal tilt to a vertigo-inducing shift.

If you use a tripod, adjust one leg so that it's shorter than the other two. If you use a laptop or desk-mounted camera, place books or some other object under your equipment. Make sure that your equipment is secure before you start shooting.

### •••Shoot•••

- ✦ Confide your most embarrassing moment. What made it so difficult? How does it feel to confess it to your camera?

- ✦ Alternatively, is there a part of your life that feels out of balance? It could be that work or school life intrudes on home life. Or perhaps you wish you had more space for creative pursuits.

- ✦ First, talk about the facts: Why does your life feel out of balance? Then, talk about the feelings: How does the lack of balance affect you?

*Good art is art that allows you to enter it from a variety of angles and to emerge with a variety of views.*

**—Mary Schmich**

### ▲Replay▲

- ❖ Review your embarrassing moment. Other people have no doubt forgotten your foible—they have plenty of their own.

- ❖ Did telling it to your camera diffuse the feelings or intensify them?

## Upside Down:

This angle isn't used often but is powerful when it's done well. One example is a haunting sequence from *Apocalypse Now*. The burning jungle is juxtaposed with an upside down view of Martin Sheen, smoking a cigarette. The scene dissolves from a shot of helicopter blades to a rotating ceiling fan above Sheen, still upside down, as he lies in bed.

Shooting upside down can be challenging. Either the camera needs to be upside down or you do. If you use a laptop with a built-in camera, you may have no choice but to become Bat Person. Turn the laptop so that the screen and keyboard face away from you. Stand up and lean over to face upside down into you camera. Not the most comfortable position, but you'll get the desired effect.

If you're shooting with a small USB camera or camcorder, you can either hang over the camera so that you are upside down or flip the camera. You might want to try both to see how each feels. With a camcorder you can also hold the camera out in front of you and orientate it.

*Every man takes the limits of his own field of vision for the limits of the world.*

**—Arthur Schopenhauer**

### •••Shoot•••

Pick a moment in your life when everything changed. It could have been a temporary change or permanent.

- ✦ Talk about the first time you fell in love. Who did you fall in love with? What impact did they have on your life then? How about now? Envision that they are on the other side of the lens.

- ✦ Talk about a major life change. It could be a cross-country move, career promotion, new school, break up, or a milestone birthday. Who were you then compared to now? Is there a core, essential part of you that remains the same no matter what? See if you can speak from that inner core of stillness amidst the inevitable changes (and even though you are hanging upside down!).

## Handheld:

Shooting handheld may not be possible depending on your set-up. If you use a camcorder or digital still camera, it's easy. The major advantage to handheld is freedom. You can make an entry as you walk. You can put the camera in your lap, or hold it high above your head.

**•••Shoot•••**

- ✦ If you have a portable camera, record yourself while you walk through your home. Hold your arm out straight but relaxed and slightly downward and point the camera at your face. Talk about a time when you felt limitless freedom to be yourself. If you haven't had this experience, try to create it now.

Shooting handheld gives an interesting perspective because the camera travels with your body. It's the most flexible way of shooting (though can be physically tiring) and gives videos a fun immediacy. If it gets too shaky, though, it can be distracting and tiring to watch.

You'll find that you get better with practice and you just might develop new muscles as well. Who needs a gym when you have a camera?

*Freedom requires that you discover your own inner language, your own life rules, your own vision.*

**—Zephyr Bloch-Jorgensen**

## —Background: Your Rear View—

People frequently don't pay much attention to what's behind them when they shoot. However, your background has an emotional as well as aesthetic impact. For this exercise, watch yourself on-screen rather than looking directly in the lens.

**•••Shoot•••**

- ✦ Find a visually busy background. It could be a garage or a corner of your home that needs organizational TLC. Make a spontaneous one-minute entry talking about *your* background, for example:

ethnicity, where you grew up or whatever aspects the visuals of the location trigger.

- ✦ Find or make a colorful backdrop with plenty of texture. Create a one-minute entry on the effect that your background has had on the texture of your life. For example, you might explore traditions unique to your upbringing that still affect you today.

- ✦ Find a sparse backdrop to shoot against such as a white wall. Make a one-minute entry on the influences you've left behind, whether intentionally or unintentionally.

### ▲Replay▲

- ❖ Notice the reactions the locations provoke in you as you watch. How do the backgrounds compare in the way they affect you?

*We are linked by blood, and blood is memory without language.*

**—Joyce Carol Oates**

- ❖ Did the backgrounds affect what you ended up speaking about?

Video bloggers often place backdrops behind them. Sometimes this is a neutral piece of black or white fabric. Other times it is a specially colored fabric or painted surface called a green screen or blue screen.

With the right software and proper lighting you can replace, or "key out," the blue or green screen and add a new background. From the Eiffel Tower to the Sahara Desert, whatever you can dream up you can place behind you digitally. For a simple version, try iMovie, but for pro results you'll need software like Final Cut Pro or Adobe Premiere.

Note that if you plan to upload your footage online, simple backdrops tend to work better. During the upload process, footage is compressed and busy areas tend to lose detail quickly.

This brings us to the close of *Week Five*. Next week you'll go deeper into your history, examine the patterns that make up your life and create a video time capsule.

*Week Six Notes:*

# Week Six
## Leave a Legacy: Recapture Your History

History is described as: "acts, ideas, or events that will or can shape the course of the future" according to one definition.[1] Using video to explore your history offers the chance to understand the past, reclaim the present and find direction for the future. It can also allow others to learn from your unique life path.

### —Family History—

*If you want to understand today, you have to search yesterday.*

**—Pearl S. Buck**

Perhaps you've had the experience of finding a photo album left behind by a relative and not knowing the circumstances surrounding the images. You don't need to subject others to this frustration. Using today's technology you can leave behind an extraordinarily rich family history for future generations.

Whether it's five or fifty years from now (presuming you've arranged to preserve your footage—we'll get to this in *Part Four*) anyone will be able to view the photos and enjoy the stories surrounding them.

#### •••Shoot•••

✦ Go through your old photos on-camera and elaborate on them. This will help jog your memory and allow future audiences to envision what you're describing.

✦ If you feel ambitious, import digital versions into your video using software like iMovie or Window's Movie Maker.

✦ Recall stories that your mother, father, or grandparents have told you about their lives. These could range from the dinner table anecdotes of mom's colorful childhood, or granddad's recollections of Vietnam or the Korean War.

- ✦ Relate your own stories from the past—conversations, incidents and adventures with mothers, fathers, brothers, sisters, uncles, and aunts. Be sure to include humorous or difficult incidents and plenty of detail to bring them to life.

## —The Story of Objects—

Choose an object that has deep meaning to you. Generally items you've owned for longer will have more of a story to tell. Perhaps it's an article of clothing given to you by a favorite aunt or a grandparent. It might be something you bought on a vacation where you learned a new skill like surfing or speaking Spanish. Or it could be an item with a painful memory attached, like a gift from a past boyfriend or girlfriend that was never discarded. If it has meaning to you and a story you'd like to relate, it will work perfectly.

*A hidden connection is stronger than an obvious one.*
**—Heraclitus of Ephesus**

### •••Shoot•••

- ✦ Tell the story of your object, and don't censor if something seemingly random comes up.

- ✦ Objects often have hidden stories that emerge. Go with this. If you're unsure what something you're saying means, record it anyway. You can always revisit it later.

- ✦ Don't forget to hold the item up so that your camera can see it. Try to keep the object in the shot with you while you speak.

You could record an entire series of objects this way, perhaps even an entire room in your home. This might lead to an extensive video history or a personal documentary on a hobby or collection of items that you've gathered over the years. Be prepared for meanings and connections to emerge that you never realized existed.

## —Your Legacy—

Thousands of years ago people left their legacy in the form of something called an "ethical will." These were originally oral records common in traditions ranging from Judaism to Christianity to Islam. Ethical wills connected people to their cultural history and allowed them to pass on their values to future generations. Despite its roots in the oral tradition, the ethical will became better known as a written document. Now with video, the ethical will has, in a way, come full circle.

There is no recipe for recording an ethical will. They are a unique expression of each individual. You may want to create more than one, or continue adding to an ongoing ethical will as you travel through life. The only essential thing is that your will comes from the heart.

### •••Shoot•••

*Here is the test to find whether your mission on Earth is finished: if you're alive, it isn't.*

**—Richard Bach**

As a general guideline, consider the following as you video:

- ✦ What are your personal credos, values, and beliefs?
- ✦ What are some lessons you've learned in life?
- ✦ What would you want the people you love to know if, (insert your higher power of choice here) forbid, you were hit by a falling anvil tomorrow?
- ✦ Who would you like to forgive or ask forgiveness from?
- ✦ What are your experiences of love gained and love lost?

This isn't meant to be a morbid exercise. Ethical wills are as much about maintaining current perspective so you can live fully *now* as they are leaving your legacy for a distant future.

## —Time-Lapsed Life—

Several video bloggers have taken digital still photos of themselves over a period of time—six years, eight years—then combined them into one video. One of the first was the YouTube video *Noah takes a photo of himself every day for 6 years*. The effect can be dramatic and moving. Incidentally, Noah plans on taking a photo of himself every day for the rest of his life. Consider how you might shoot your own time-lapse creations. Following are several ideas to try.

### •••Shoot•••

✦ Videotape a thirty-second clip of the same daily activity for seven days (or more) in a row. For example, this could be brushing your teeth, drying your hair, dressing for work, etc.

✦ Record the same view from your window for one full year. Limit the entry to two seconds and say one word that describes how you feel. At the end of the year you will have an approximately twelve-minute piece. By the way, two seconds is long enough for just about any word—but if you need longer for the occasional "supercalifragilicious-expealidocious"—go for it.

*Every activity belongs to a pattern. You identify with your pattern or thought. Your patterns lead your life.*

**—J.G. Gallimore**

✦ Record one entry per day for three seconds when you first wake up or right before bed. Speak directly to your camera. Keep the same format for each entry, for example: "This morning I feel <BLANK>," or "My day today was <BLANK>."

✦ Incorporate the tone of your voice and facial expression to embody your feelings regarding that day.

### ▲Replay▲

❖ Reviewing the patterns that make up our lives can be revealing (not to mention humbling at times).

❖ Try to remain unbiased. What would your impressions be if you didn't know the person you viewed?

❖ What aspects of your life escaped your attention until you recorded them in succession?

## —Nightly News—

There's an old saying that history gets written by those who record it. In the past, large events in history were only seen through the lens of mass media. Before mass media, history was recorded by the privileged few who were literate. Then the individuals who had access to the grand institutions of the period doled out information on their terms.

Imagine a distant time from now. A relative of yours—it could be a child, grandchild or perhaps a friend of the family—is writing a report on the first African American president. Not only do they research archived news from the era, they are able to see, listen, and hear *your* impressions and feelings.

*99.99% of what happens is not on the news.*

**—Loesje**

You'd allow them to personalize history, connect to it, and bring it to life. In the recent past, only the rich or technologically advanced could afford to do something like this. Today it's open to just about anyone. Your *Nightly News* may also become a video blog that you share with the world. There will be more on this in *Week Eight*.

### •••Shoot•••

Create your own nightly news broadcast on a topic or topics of importance to you. They can be global or from right at home. Here are some ideas:

✦ Watch the news (either online or on TV, but best if it's prerecorded so you can hit "pause") and record your own commentary. Are they on target or off base?

- Go through a local newspaper or online news source such as a blog, and editorialize on-camera.

- Give a news report about your neighborhood. What are some of the things going on that an outsider would never notice?

- Get very local. Give a news report about the goings-on in your household. This might be something that you end up sharing.

- Shamelessly editorialize. Highlight the aspects important to the subject, even if they aren't what others tend to focus on.

## —Video Gifting—

Record a personal message for a close friend or family member. If it's for their birthday, you can give this to them instead of a card—or if you package it nicely (a decorated DVD or USB thumb drive for example), make it your gift to them. It doesn't need to be for a birthday, though. It could be for any occasion, or a spontaneous act of kindness.

*If you don't like the news, go out and make some of your own.*

**—Wes Nisker**

If you have children, dictate a birthday message on each birthday year until they are eighteen, then give them a compilation. Each entry should be one to three minutes, five minutes tops.

In the video, you might want to tell them what's going on for you in your life, what's going on in the world, and what their life is like at that moment.

## —Video Time Capsule—

Westinghouse created the first modern "time bomb" (wisely renamed time capsule) for the 1939 World's Fair in New York. Everyday items ranging from a fountain pen to children's toys to movie reels of the period were included.

The capsule is slated to be opened fifty centuries from its creation, in the year 6939. It even includes an instructional key to the English language in case we no longer speak it by then.

Create your own time capsule to be viewed on a certain date. No need for fifty centuries. The time capsule could be for you or for someone else to discover. One year from now, five years from now, on New Year's Day or on your birthday are all good possibilities.

### •••Shoot•••

*The only reason for time is so that everything doesn't happen at once.*

**—Albert Einstein**

- ✦ Describe where you are now in your life and give some advice to your "future self."
- ✦ What would you like your future self to be aware of?
- ✦ Record some of the things you want to accomplish.
- ✦ Include some cultural markers of your everyday life: your favorite music, the movies you watch, the activities you enjoy with friends.

We've achieved a lot up to this point and now it's time to change direction slightly. It's comfortable recording a video journal or blog in your home environment, but there's a whole world outside waiting to be explored. Next week you'll have the chance to do just that.

*Week Seven Notes:*

# Week Seven
## Location Shooting: Challenge Comfort Zones

Once you're comfortable recording yourself indoors it's time to head outdoors. This might mean an entry reflecting on nature during a long secluded walk or while hanging out in your backyard. It could also mean a busy park or a shopping mall. The places are only limited by your imagination and comfort.

If you don't have a mobile camera set-up, it won't be possible to do some of the following exercises. Modify them for your situation as best you can, or spring for a cheap portable camera.

Making an entry where other people can watch you (and some will be curious) may be challenging initially. But it can also push through boundaries. Life is too short to worry about what other people think. Determine the edge of your comfort level and explore that.

*Be who you are and say what you feel because those who mind don't matter and those who matter don't mind.*

**—Dr. Seuss**

While outside, consider shooting your surroundings (the people and places), and include this as part of the entry. One caveat however, the logistics of the place in question should be kept in mind.

In general, individuals well in the background of parks, public streets, beaches and the like are okay. If you're shooting close-ups of people and plan on posting the video online, you may want to get written permission in the form of a release. A release gives formal written permission for you to use their image. There is a sample included at www.nakedlensbook.com in the "resources" section.

The Internet is still a bit of a grey area in this regard. Most video bloggers don't bother with releases and tend not to incur any legal hassles, but that might change in the future. Some video bloggers have been offered opportunities to license their videos but weren't able to because they lacked necessary permissions.

If you're using the video privately, officially you don't need releases or permission in a public place, even if it makes someone uncomfortable. Unless you have good reason though, it's generally not cool to record someone against their wish. If you're ultra intrusive, you might even end up with a broken camera or worse, so be careful out there.

No doubt you figured out that the gym locker room or hospital waiting area might get less than enthusiastic responses. Since 9/11 some previously okay areas have also become iffy. For example, in New York City it's no longer allowable to shoot in the subway system or on the city's bridges without permission. In fact, the NYPD pulled me over as I shot video of the Brooklyn Bridge from the open window of a taxicab. I was told to stop or have my camera confiscated. Who knew?

## —Walk Back in Time—

Visit a neighborhood from your past; it could be where you grew up, a place where you lived, an area that you used to work in, or even the site of a historic occurrence that is personal to you, such as your high school graduation.

*There is nothing like returning to a place that remains unchanged to find the ways in which you yourself have altered.*

**—Nelson Mandela**

### •••Shoot•••

✦ Record your memories and impressions as you stroll past your old haunts (or do so when you return home).

✦ What has changed and what has remained the same?

✦ What's it like being back on these streets?

✦ Pay attention to the specific cues that jog memories. Are they sounds, sights, smells, or perhaps even tastes? How might they be expressed on video?

✦ Were you the same person then as you are now? How do you define this?

If you don't have the type of camera that you can travel to your neighborhood with (such as a laptop), here's an alternative. Gather some photos of the neighborhood and hold them up to show the camera.

Or shoot current digital photos and hold the camera up and video the LCD screen. As you show each photo, speak about the neighborhood and talk about the time and place the photo was taken.

If your technical skills are more advanced, scan in some old photos of your neighborhood. Digital photos can be easily imported as JPEGs, BMPs and other digital formats and combined with your footage using programs such as iMovie or Windows Movie Maker.

## —Including Others—

Up until now you have created your video journal or video blog on your own. There are many ways you can include other people, depending on your goals and comfort level. It's not possible to go into all of them, but here are a few ideas.

*He who controls others may be powerful, but he who has mastered himself is mightier still.*

**—Lao Szu**

### •••Shoot•••

✦ Choose one of the exercises from the preceding weeks, and make an entry with a friend or family member. Do this somewhere outdoors if you like. Be clear about why you want to include them and whether it will be part of your private video journal or a public video blog. For example, you could choose the *Video Self-Portrait* exercise in *Week Four* and make a joint portrait.

✦ Allow a friend or family member to interview you with your camera. I generally recommend against having someone else record you when you make your entries. The magic of addressing your camera directly is that you address "yourself"—which is both powerful and rarely experienced. However, being interviewed by someone is interesting as a comparison.

✦ Switch roles so that you are the interviewer and the other person is the interviewee. If you notice a sense of power or being in control, where does it come from?

- Talk about this and reverse roles again. See if you can maintain your sense of presence no matter which side of the lens you are on.

## —Out-of-Town Guest—

Choose a place that you go to regularly (local bar, beach, restaurant, family or friend's house, etc.), and bring your camera along as if it were an out-of-town guest.

### •••Shoot•••

- Narrate where you are going and why.

- Introduce friends and people you meet along the way on-camera.

- Notice how it feels to speak to your camera in public. If you feel awkward, try to determine why. For example, do you want not to stand out? Fear others' judgments? Is there a valid reason for these feelings or are they self-created?

*Communication leads to community, that is, to understanding, intimacy and mutual valuing.*

**—Rollo May**

- Allow your camera to be passed around. Have others (including yourself) make their own entries, in front of the group or off on their own. Encourage everyone to participate. If you like, edit this together and share it.

- Remember to stay present and in the moment. Bringing a camera *will* change your experience.

- If you become too caught up in technical details or the process of shooting, it may have a negative impact.

- If you integrate your camera with the experience and allow it to *increase* the intensity of your being in each moment, it should be a very positive one.

## ✪ Life as Story ✪

In *Week Two*, you told your story one-on-one to your camera. Now you have the chance to experiment further. There are countless ways to tell a story visually, but here is one exercise to get you started.

### •••Shoot•••

"Once upon a time" stories are the most familiar variety of story for most people. Like classic fables and fairy tales, they have a clear beginning, middle, and end. These stories also have clear protagonists, in other words, the person we identify with.

For our purposes, the protagonist will be you. (You could also make a video blog about someone else or have a friend act out a script you wrote, but that isn't what we'll cover. The general principles would remain the same, though.)

*A man would do nothing if he waited until he could do it so well that no one could find fault.*

**—John Henry Newman**

Decide on an activity you'd like to video. It could be a visit to a family member you haven't seen in a while, going on a hike or even something mundane like cleaning your garage. It doesn't matter what the activity is, as long as it is meaningful and interesting to you.

For now, let's assume that you won't edit your material later. Whatever you record will be left as is. Choosing not to edit frees you up to go with whatever happens. The "mistakes" you make often become the most interesting parts.

✦ **Record your set-up.** The set-up introduces you, the protagonist. This could be an on-screen intro to camera, or a visual moment that defines an aspect of who you are. (For example, you decide to shoot your first swim of the year in the ocean. Perhaps you video yourself checking the weather, calling a friend to arrange it, or you just tell us: "Hey, I'm off to have my first swim of the year!")

✦ **Next, record the question or goal that your story will answer or fulfill.** The goal usually arises from the reason that you chose to shoot in the first place. (For example, you video a selection of bathing suits, and tell your camera that none fit so you'll buy a new one on the way to the beach. Now the goal becomes buying a bathing suit you love.) If you haven't decided why you're videoing, then theoretically, discovering that can become your goal. By the end of the day hopefully you discover your reason.

- **Now, record your journey.** This is the body of your story. It includes all the activities that lead up to the conclusion. Will you or won't you achieve your goal? (For example—in our imaginary situation—will you or won't you find the perfect swimsuit and take your first dip of the year?)

- **Once you feel that your goal has (or has not) been attained, find a way to wrap things up.** This might be an on-camera summary or it could be one image that encapsulates your day. (For example, if you go swimming, then your conclusion could be testing the water temperature with a toe and shooting your reaction. If you have a waterproof video camera, next you dive in. If you don't go swimming because you can't find a suit, walking out of the store while you fume about your troubles is just as good a conclusion, even though you didn't achieve your initial goal.)

*The life of every man is a diary in which he means to write one story, and writes another.*
**—James Matthew Barrie**

That's it! You've introduced yourself, set up your situation and allowed it to run to its inevitable conclusion. The example above is a simple story, but it has all the basic elements. The complexity of yours is up to you.

Most people who shoot stories like this end up posting them in a video blog. You can also make these stories as video journal entries for yourself. There are various reasons you might do this—from the sheer fun of creative expression to working through an issue that's been bothering you. Okay, now get out there and try it.

## —Video Scrapbook—

Video scrapbooks take the idea of linear storytelling from the former exercise and toss it out. Just like its physical counterpart, the video version of the scrapbook is your opportunity to take random "pieces" of your life and create a greater whole from the parts.

### •••Shoot•••

- ✦ This exercise works best with a small, portable camera. Carry your camera with you at all times during the week.

- ✦ Shoot anything that catches your eye. This could be part of a conversation you have, an interesting building, a street scene, or your dog's antics—whatever grabs your attention. Take short bites, five or ten seconds is perfect, but no more than fifteen seconds.

*A story should have a beginning, a middle, and an end...but not necessarily in that order.*

**—Jean-Luc Godard**

- ✦ Remain strict about the fifteen-second limit. You will often have to stop shooting "in the middle" of something. These interruptions are one of the points of the exercise.

- ✦ By letting the video camera capture these moments, you can relax your perception and let what happens in the viewfinder flow past without needing to remember or become attached. Pay attention to each recorded second and see how this shifts perception.

- ✦ You may get the urge to create a story, to shape and direct what you're filming. Resist this impulse. Shoot each moment for the sake of the moment itself.

### ▲Replay▲

- ❖ Notice how the interruptions affect you as the viewer. Often they paradoxically increase interest and engagement.

- Do these moments highlight an aspect of your day that you didn't notice as you lived it?
- Does your material tell its own story even if not narrative?
- Perhaps you recorded a friend's tirade next to your dog's barking, or the flowing architectural lines of a building create a jarring visual contrast to the tumbling dance of a street performer.

## —Back to Nature—

Taking your camera into nature offers you the chance to observe a different rhythm. This could mean visiting a national park or a forest, but it might also be close to home. From backyards to city parks, to green patches on urban boulevards and birds in the sky, nature surrounds us when we pause and look.

*When you take a flower in your hand and really look at it, it's your world for the moment. I want to give that world to someone else.*

**—Georgia O'Keeffe**

### •••Shoot•••

- Choose a location and visit it regularly over a set period. Place your camera in the same location each time (a tripod will help). Observe how the location changes over the period. You may also like to come back over four different seasons.
- Find somewhere quiet like a park. Sit silently and take a few three-part breaths. Remain mindful and aware. Experience yourself as part of the environment. Use your camera to convey the experience this invokes. Allow it to be as abstract as it needs to. For example, it could be that you move your camera in harmony with the pattern of tree branches swaying in a breeze.
- Visit your favorite outdoor location. Choose an animal such as a bird, or it could even be an insect. Observe them until you form

a connection and begin to understand them better. Use your camera to convey the world as you imagine they experience it.

**▲Replay▲**

- Review your material and see if you can reconnect with the rhythm you connected to in nature, back at home.

## —The Open Road—

A video travel journal is an excellent way of keeping a travel log that is packed full of rich and evocative memories. It is also something that others will likely find entertaining (unlike your standard travel video).

Many travel videos contain long pans over static objects—statues, buildings and landmarks. Missing is a unique perspective and point of view. However, this is generally what people want to see.

*The real voyage of discovery consists not in seeking new landscapes but in having new eyes.*
**—Marcel Proust**

Matthew Harding, also known as "Dancing Matt," became well known for his videos that feature him dancing in various locations around the globe. The videos started as an in-joke between friends and family but quickly exploded in popularity. Once he became known, people often joined him in dancing by the hundreds. He was even hired by Visa for their *Travel Happy* campaign.

If you find yourself struggling with what to say—don't worry—just keep talking (or start dancing). If you free-associate you'll get into a groove. Besides, people love to watch other people struggle on-camera. The authenticity is what's important. No matter what, it will still be a snapshot of where you were in life at that moment in time.

I also recommend recording an entry once you're back in your accommodations. Be sure to record the room itself. In Marcel Proust's autobiographical novel *In Search of Lost Time*, the author is launched into a vivid stream of childhood memory provoked by the mere taste of a *madeleine*—a local dessert dipped in tea.

This "involuntary memory" is precious because it's unpredictable. Speaking from personal experience, the street sounds of a noisy Beijing hotel room brought back not only memories of the trip but precisely how I felt at that time.

Further, this entry offers the chance for quiet reflection. Dive deep and record your thoughts and feelings once the day is over.

## —Spiritual Electricity—

Use whatever term fits for you—God, Buddha nature, higher consciousness, or higher self—"spirit" holds a unique place when it comes to creativity and self-transformation. Creative energy is often referred to as a kind of "spiritual electricity."[1] Since this book focuses on using electronic video technology for self-exploration, this feels appropriate. Further, society's relationship to technology often ignores this aspect.

*In order to achieve their potentials, spirituality needs digital technology and digital technology needs spirituality.*[2]

**—H.H. Dalai Lama**

Spirituality attempts to answer the question as to what the ultimate meaning of our existence is. It encompasses aspects of life ranging from our relationships with self and the world to our inner and outer goals. Many write in journals to connect to spirit. Video can be used in the same way.

People sometimes get nervous when "spiritual" is spoken in the same breath as "technology," and this isn't a new fear. In the 1600s, there was an outcry when Bibles were duplicated via the printing press rather than written out by hand. But today a person would be laughed at if they suggested that books or printing technology were incompatible with spiritual aspirations. A video camera may seem a much different technology than a book, but it's a matter of perception.

Books are tools that communicate, and so is video. A video camera may seem high-tech, but its materials have been around since the birth of our planet. The glass of the camera lens is nothing but powdered limestone sand combined with the mineral sodium carbonate. The plastic casing is made up of long atomic chains of carbon, hydrogen and oxygen. We humans created video to improve our ability to communicate. Its incredible capabilities indicate the strength of this urge to connect with one another.

### •••Shoot•••

- ✦ Take a deep, three-part breath and center yourself. Remain mindful, and take as long as you need for this exercise.
- ✦ Connect to whatever you consider to be your "source" of energy and creativity.
- ✦ Gaze at your camera, and remember that it is made of the same basic elements as yourself. Close your eyes. Ask this source what purpose the camera fills in your life.
- ✦ Be open to this answer being completely different from what you originally thought when you started the workshop or from the everyday meanings of video technology.
- ✦ Close your eyes and describe any images that appear. Or, an answer might come in the form of an intuition or creative idea.
- ✦ Once you feel like you've reached a natural conclusion, open your eyes and record any other thoughts that occurred.

*The point is not what you name it. The point is that you try using it. For many of us, thinking of it as a form of spiritual electricity has been a very useful jumping-off place.*

**—Julia Cameron**

### ▲Replay▲

- ❖ If you watch your entry and feel you weren't able to connect *because* of the camera, explore this further.
- ❖ Your camera is high-tech, probably shiny and has corporate branding on it. But that's just its appearance. See if you can get beyond the way a camera looks. What you record becomes its essence. Without you, it's just a bunch of atoms stuck together.

This brings us to the end of *Week Seven*. In our next and final week, there will be the chance to experiment with video as art and we'll look at four *different* ways to go public by video blogging. It's not all or nothing.

*Week Eight Notes:*

# Week Eight
## That's (Almost) a Wrap: Now What?

You've achieved a lot over the past weeks. Look back at some of your entries. Allow yourself to appreciate your accomplishments.

This is also the point to reconsider your goals. Will you continue making a daily private video journal entry? If you aren't already, perhaps you want to share your work with others through a video blog? Would you like to try making some videos that are more experimental in nature?

In this final week, we explore all of the above.

### ✪ Experiments in Video & Life ✪

*Find something only you can say.*
**—James Dickey**

Experimental video blogs tend to use images and unexpected juxtapositions to create a mood or communicate an idea. They are more reliant on images, music and sound. You can include yourself in the imagery or you might use other people, architecture or any other object you can think of. In this section we'll look at video art, visual poems and a second opportunity to create a self-portrait.

**Video Art:**

Video art pushes boundaries of the mainstream, explores video as pure creative expression, and challenges the expectations that viewers have of video and art. For example, video blogger Jay Dedman begins with an extremely tight close-up of an abstract reflection of sunlight in a cup of coffee during his *CoffeeBlog* piece. This is juxtaposed with poetic musings on existence as he widens to reveal his location.[1] However, this is just one example. Video art is difficult to describe or define because it is extremely subjective. The best way to understand it is to create it.

**•••Shoot•••**

- When you think of video art, what do you see in your mind's eye?

- Is there anything that you couldn't express during the past weeks—a long-held secret or a painful emotion? Consider bringing this out in an abstract, artistic sense. Self-expression on video doesn't necessarily mean going into specific details. It can be deeply cathartic to represent something metaphorically and release it that way.

- What do you have a difficult time expressing to people in words? Allow your mind to wander, and see if image fragments appear that relate to these.

- Sometimes images in our mind's eye are easy to capture on video. Other times we need to modify their expression.

- Don't be afraid to change your idea to fit your abilities. It will often become even stronger.

*Art is the only way to run away without leaving home.*

**—Twyla Tharp**

**Visual Poetry:**

Choose a poem either that you wrote or that resonates with you. This is your chance to use images to express the poem's meaning without the need for them to make sense on a rational level.

**•••Shoot•••**

- Either record yourself speaking the poem and add images that go along with it, or compose a visual poem entirely from images in response to the words.

- What visual images "rhyme" with one another similar to the way that words do? What rhymes with a sunset? A close-up of your eye? An old man raking autumn leaves? This is your poem, so you make the connections with no right or wrong answers.

- ✦ Feel free to add music and sound. Remember that if music has a copyright (most does) and the video is posted online, there could be complications. However, there is "fair use" in artistic expression. For more on this important issue, check out www.nakedlensbook.com.

**Video Portrait Take Two:**

There were certain constrictions imposed during your first video portrait. Make a second video portrait imposing your own structure. Play to the strengths that you've uncovered during the workshop.

*Poetry is just the evidence of life. If your life is burning well, poetry is just the ash.*

**—Leonard Cohen**

**•••Shoot•••**

I recommend defining *some* structure to follow because this often stimulates creativity. For instance, you could make a video portrait of "you" five years from now. Here are some other possibilities:

- ✦ Make a portrait using "staged moments." For example, set your camera on a tripod and video yourself walking through a park or riding your bike. Recreate aspects of your life that are the most emblematic and then set them to music.

- ✦ Is there an important incident from your life that you'd like to revisit? Brainstorm simple ways of recreating it. Enlist friends to help if you like.

- ✦ Consider ways you might use extreme close-ups of objects to disrupt notions of space and time in your video. Use only close-ups or wide-shots, for example.

- Rather than speaking directly to your camera, record the entry silently. Concentrate on close-ups of your face and impressionistic images, and then add a voiceover later. (This will require editing—see *Chapter 11*.)

## —Public or Private?—

The writer Thomas Mallon calls the journal "the record of a soul's journey." Mallon suggests that no one keeps a diary just for himself or herself. Keeping a journal signifies the need to connect to someone or something else or maybe even to oneself.[2] The same can be said for the video journal.

In a world infused with visual images from myriad sources, we now have the chance to create images our own way. Experimenting and playing with video is an opportunity to assert our sense of self in defiance of the mainstream media's definition of who we may (or may not) be. It's also an opportunity to be heard and hopefully understood.

*He that writes to himself writes to an eternal public.*

**—Ralph Waldo Emerson**

### Making the Choice:

"On the other side of that little glass dot is everyone who is." This is the way new media anthropologist Michael Wesch describes sitting in front of a webcam.[3] Choosing whether to go public with your material is not a decision to be made lightly. But neither should it be avoided—because it's an unprecedented opportunity. That said, some of the videos posted on YouTube make me wonder if the people posting them thought it through.

People often falsely believe that they have complete control over videos they upload. They think that if they decide to remove their video blog, they'll easily be able to do so. Unfortunately, this isn't always possible. Videos can be extracted from one site and copied to another. If a video grows popular, it may become impossible to remove from the Internet completely.

Emily Gould is a blogger who recently wrote about her blogging experience in *The New York Times Magazine.* Gould shared numerous personal details in her blog, *Emily Magazine,* and it gained many followers. As it grew in popularity, she experienced what she called "negative scrutiny" which ultimately prompted her to go into therapy. From what I understand, she continues to maintain her blog, but her situation still presents a good cautionary tale. She pushed herself beyond her comfort zone.

Anything that is made public on the Net, be it a written blog or video blog, *might* become more popular than originally planned. For many people, unexpected popularity is a best-case scenario, but it's a good idea to think it through first. Consider the audience of people who might see your video, and then rate your comfort level. Imagine the following scenarios:

*Live each moment like it's the last, and do each task like it's the first.*

**—Quincy Jones**

- ➜ A friend or family member sees it.
- ➜ A work or school colleague sees it.
- ➜ An acquaintance or a friend you've fallen out of touch with views it.
- ➜ Many thousands or even millions of strangers see it.

If you're comfortable with the above, then release yourself to the Net. If you have any reservations, either make changes to address them, or give it a few days before you upload the video. I recommend that first-timers "sleep on it" before posting any but the most innocuous material.

On the other hand, it's not necessary to feel completely comfortable with all the above scenarios before you post a video. For example, you might feel uncomfortable about your colleagues viewing your video blog. Unless you believe that you'd be fired if your workmates saw the video, the worst-case scenario is that you would feel uncomfortable. And there are far worse things than that.

The reality is that out of hundreds of thousands of videos, it is unlikely anyone you know will stumble across yours unless you want them to. This can be considered low risk, high reward. We've all felt uncomfortable before and lived to eat a new bowl of cornflakes. Added to this are the many reasons to make a public video blog. Reasons such as:

- ➜ Communicate your story/thoughts/personal creativity to others who will be affected in ways both large and small by having viewed them.
- ➜ Connect with people from around the world that share common interests or have a similar outlook on life.
- ➜ Make difficult feelings or life situations public as a form of release or to help others going through the same experience.
- ➜ Create positive change by video blogging on the many challenges our world faces.
- ➜ Promote a good or service you offer.
- ➜ Share your talents with a massive audience and perhaps even be broadly "discovered" if that's your goal.
- ➜ Make a full-time career of video blogging if you find that it's something you have a passion for.
- ➜ Join the video revolution and become a part of its evolution.

*Isn't privacy about keeping taboos in their place?*

**—Kate Millett**

Many people assume that either you create a public video blog for the world to see, or that you create a private video journal for yourself. But out in the real world, there are many shades of grey. According to what I've found and an interesting study by Patricia Lange at the University of Southern California[4], there are several approaches that video blogging tends to follow.

## Staying Private:

As mentioned earlier, there is a subtle (or not so subtle) expectation that private video entries will ultimately be made into public video blogs. If it's helpful, keeping your entire endeavor secret will shield you from unwanted pressure.

Keeping certain videos private allows the space to experiment and venture into emotional and creative territory that you might not otherwise. As you review your videos, you might find some you want to turn into a video blog, and others you would never even consider.

There might also be sections of videos that you'd like to make public, in which case an edit might be appropriate. But going public doesn't need to be all-or-nothing.

## Fully Public:

*At this very moment, there are people only you can reach... And differences only you can make.*

**—Mike Dooley**

A fully public video is a video blog posted using your real name or email with the intent that as many people see it as possible. These videos will often show up in a Google search of your name whether done by friends, family members or potential employers. Generally, no matter how comfortable you are, it's unwise to give too many identifying details.

As an example of someone who chose to be very public, Luke Johnson performed an interesting experiment on YouTube. He gave his phone number out online to see how many people would call him. He had millions of hits and in the end over 130,000 people called him from around the world. Recently I tried to give him a call to see how things were going but his number was disconnected. Hopefully, he had plenty of minutes in his cell phone plan.

## Privately Public:

Unless you use your real name or recognizable email as your online identity, the chances that your video blog will be seen by someone you know out of the many thousands available is unlikely. Of course, it could happen if your video becomes wildly popular, so you should consider this. Emmalina, mentioned in *Week Two*, chose the above route. Her video blogs are quite personal but she keeps her real name private. For Emmalina, the anonymity gives her the chance to experiment with different points of view, which may not reflect her everyday self. She has kept some privacy while enjoying a public presence.

### Publicly Private:

In this scenario, you release your video blog widely but obscure your identity. Some people use dim lighting, back lighting, or even a mask. It's possible that your identity will somehow be discovered, but it's unlikely if you do it right. People also do this to create a specific character.

MadV is (presumably) a male who created a character that uses pantomime instead of speech and wears a Guy Fawkes mask. In one video he takes off his mask, but he uses computer-generated effects to render nothing but a black hole under his hoodie. This doesn't necessarily prevent making a connection to viewers. MadV asked people to write a response on their hands referring to the video's theme of "one world." *One World* became one of the most responded to videos ever.

*There is no such thing as bad publicity except your own obituary.*
**—Brendan Behan**

### Selectively Private:

Most video sharing sites allow videos to be defined as "friends only." This is perfect for videos that you share only with immediate friends and family, with one caveat. Make sure you understand the way the website functions. If you mess up and define a video as "public" rather than "private," you may be in for a surprise.

### Others' Privacy:

You may be completely comfortable out there for the world to see, but your friends and family may not. Be sensitive to others' needs for privacy and you'll save yourself some uncomfortable conversations.

Your shy, sleep-apnea-suffering Uncle Bernie may not be thrilled that his work buddies watched him snore like a jack hammer on YouTube. This also applies to what you say about other people if it's possible they can be identified through your relationship.

Ironically, one of the top so-called viral videos resulted in a privacy lawsuit. A video featuring footage of a fourteen-year-old Canadian high school student wielding a golf ball retriever like a *Star Wars* light-saber was found by some classmates.

The classmates digitized the video and posted it to several file sharing services. Roughly nine hundred million views later, the boy's parents sued the classmates claiming that their child (now forever known as "Star Wars Kid") suffered irreparable damage to his reputation and required ongoing psychiatric care. The lawsuit was settled out of court but the video can still be easily found online.

*Human beings are not meant to lose their anonymity and privacy.*
**—Sarah Chalke**

### •••Shoot•••

- ✦ Make a one-minute video where you introduce yourself in your new public video blog.
- ✦ If you already keep a public video blog, make an entry about something you've wanted to talk about but haven't yet had the nerve.
- ✦ Put the video away. Tomorrow look at it again and either post it or make a private entry about why you chose not to.

## —Dealing with Haters—

They will criticize the way you look, the way you talk and just about any other random thing they can come up with. There is no way to please everyone, and there are people out there who will make sure you know that. They are commonly known as "haters."

Haters upset some people. Others laugh them off and even use their vitriol to increase their popularity. Haters are like wasps attracted to honey. If there's just a little bit of honey, you won't find many around, but when there is a big pot, they turn vicious.

In other words, if your video blog doesn't receive many views, you're not likely to attract haters. Once you become popular, that can change. Of course, you could turn off the comment function, but this will reduce the viewership and opportunity to interact, so it depends on your goals.

From an emotional standpoint, consider haters as an opportunity. They offer the chance to witness how you react to criticism. Create an entry about your feelings if you become upset. A video blogger named Paperlilies made a humorous video where she read out a long litany of nasty comments she received for one of her videos. She called it: *Hater Comments from the Sarcasm Video.* In the end, your video blogs are an opportunity to express yourself no matter what anyone else might say.

*If you have no critics you'll likely have no success.*

**—Malcolm X**

## —Ways to Go Public—

Nine motionless years. That's how much time is spent sitting watching television over the average American lifespan, and it's rising. Studies have shown that when watching TV, viewer's thoughts quiet down and the ideas presented by the TV show replace them.[5] By 2013 it's estimated the average person will spend as much time watching video content as sleeping.[6]

Unfortunately, much content is often rather cynically crafted material designed to perpetuate a mindless consumer culture. But that's slowly changing. Content is created and exchanged rather than merely consumed. People are demanding entertainment that is significant to them.

According to statistics from Internet research leader, comScore, online video is becoming a serious competitor to television.[7] Increasing numbers view their entertainment online. One compelling reason is the many options it offers. From YouTube to Yahoo! Video, from blip.tv to metacafe.com, individuals decide when, where and what to watch from thousands of options by surfing the web. No need to flip through the commercial-choked channels on TV to find something new.

What TV often lacks is true creativity—ideas with heart and spirit that inspire and encourage people rather than deadening them. There is enormous opportunity in this. If going public ignites a spark in you, explore it further. Consider what you feel passionate about. What is unique about your point of view? How might you help wake people up? If you're still not sure how (or why) to video blog, take a look at your own life.

- Do you have a unique talent or skill-set you'd like to share? Consider your own video blog series.
- Are you already a performer? Singers, comedians, and actors have all been discovered through their online work.
- Do you enjoy creating characters and playing with identity? Unleash some of your characters online. Create a venue for them.
- What are some other areas of life that inspire you? Could video fit into these in some way?
- Do you own a business? Online video is an excellent way of promoting it that has enormous untapped potential.
- When you watch the news, what are some of the goings-on that leave you seething? What might be done to create change? Give this some thought and consider making a video blog about them.
- Finally, going public doesn't mean you need to have a grand plan or idea. That is an artefact of old media. Wanting to express moments of life that are meaningful to you is as valid a reason as any.

*Talents are best nurtured in solitude, but character is best formed in the stormy billows of the world.*

**—Goethe**

Following are several ways you might choose to go public.

## Passion Pieces:

Does an important cause you're involved with crop up regularly in your video journal? Or perhaps you have a hobby that you'd like to share? Regularly keeping a journal will tend to tap into what excites you—your passions.

Valentina was a struggling artist who created *Val's Art Diary*. Since starting her online video foray, she has been featured in publications ranging from the *Wall Street Journal* to *USA Today*. Valentina has created artists' video tutorials, runs her own contests and give-aways to her online subscribers, and sells her art (including commissioned art) through her creative efforts.

## Change the World:

*Criticism is something we can avoid easily by saying nothing, doing nothing, and being nothing.*

**—Aristotle**

One way video bloggers show their passion is by creating videos to make an impact. They realize that something needs to be done to create change and so they take action. But you might say, "Oh, lots of people make videos or write blogs about 'X' issue. Do we really need another voice?" It's true; many issues have been covered, often more than once, but the more people that repeat the same messages in different ways, the more likely the balance will tip toward change.

Hank and John, the two brothers mentioned in *Chapter One*, took their unexpected online popularity and used it for good. They spawned a group called the *nerd fighters* who make it their goal to "decrease worldsuck" by getting people to donate to worthwhile causes. They ultimately partnered with Google to launch YouTube Video Volunteers, an exciting program that matches YouTubers with charities that need videos made.

Your video could show up on someone's screen just at the time they needed to see it. If your video inspires just one person, then you transform the world. There are people who need to hear your message expressed in the way only you express it. Not the way one hundred or however many other people have expressed it before you. You'll find more resources and places you can go to help make a difference at www.nakedlensbook.com.

### •••Shoot•••

Following are two broad ways to approach a change video.

1. Make a video about an issue to which you have a strong commitment and emotional connection, but that doesn't directly affect your daily life. For example, create a "rant" video voicing your anger about the situation in Afghanistan.

2. Create a video about something that directly affects you. For example, your experience as part of a minority group, as a woman, or even some direct environmental impact such as a health condition caused by local pollution.

*Never doubt that a small, group of thoughtful, committed citizens can change the world. Indeed, it is the only thing that ever has.*

**—Margaret Mead**

Within these two very broad categories, there are as many ways to create a video as there are issues. The exercises below will help get you started.

- ✦ Pick an issue that falls under the first category. Something that really bothers you. Allow yourself to vent.

- ✦ Venting sets some powerful gears in motion. If you turn it into a video blog it will connect you to others with similar passions. This could inspire new ways to further your cause and work toward change.

- ✦ Choose a topic that falls under the second category. Tell your story. Perhaps you're doing this for the first time. Take it slowly but connect to your passion and express it. You have the right to tell your own story in whatever way it needs to be told.

- ✦ Authentic personal stories, boldly told, communicate powerful messages. These can inspire change like perhaps no other method.

### ▲Replay▲

- ❖ Does your passion come across? Did you strike the right balance between expressing your passion and including the details we need to understand the situation?

- ❖ Powerful emotions can make people feel self-conscious. Take a step back and connect to your Ideal Audience from *Week Two*. Who or what did you envision if you felt self-conscious?

- ❖ Most people, even if they don't agree with someone, will respond to and respect them when they speak from their hearts. When you're ready, take a deep breath and send your work out into the world.

*On this show, your voice will be heard—in the form of my voice.*
**—Stephen Colbert**

You can also make change videos by heading out into your community and incorporating aspects of your daily life as well as the opinions of others. There is a blurry line where at some point it will become a larger project, perhaps a documentary, but I encourage you to experiment and push your own technical and creative boundaries. The following exercise treads into this area.

### Citizen Journalist:

Becoming a citizen journalist requires neither a job application nor anyone's permission. In the mainstream media model, information is created in one place (the media corporation) and sent to many (the audience). It functions as a one-way street.

With participatory media such as video blogging, formerly passive audience members inform one another. Information flows *between* individuals in often unpredictable patterns. This can lead to a snowball effect where a small story becomes big and receives widespread attention. There are several websites listed at www.nakedlensbook.com where you can upload your stories and learn more about citizen journalism.

**•••Shoot•••**

- ✦ Choose a story you want to cover. It could be something happening in your neighborhood, community, city, or an issue you've been following online.
- ✦ Consider your point of view. What needs to be said about this topic that no one has said so far?
- ✦ What emotional impact does your story have?
- ✦ Shoot a three-minute piece that expresses your viewpoint.
- ✦ Remember the "five Ws." Tell us *who* is involved, *what* is happening, *where* it is occurring, *when* it took place, and *why* we should care.

*You know, you just kind of put something silly up on YouTube and it gets lots of attention.*

**—Tay Zonday**

### Razzle Dazzle 'Em—Video Blogging to Entertain:

Creating video to entertain could mean developing a character that's emerged during the workshop. Fourteen-year-old Lucas Cruikshank created the character Fred Figglehorn primarily as a joke for his family one Halloween. Whether you find Fred endearing or annoying, Cruikshank's creation has not only proven itself to be unique, but also popular. His was the first YouTube channel to reach one million subscribers.

Singer Adam Nyerere Bahner, or "Tay Zonday" as he's known online, made a name for himself posting songs on YouTube. His best known is *Chocolate Rain*. It's a very straightforward video—Zonday stands in front of a mic and records himself on a webcam singing his song—but he's hypnotic to watch and has had millions of views.

Chris Crocker became widely known for his *Leave Britney Alone* video where he sobs violently because of criticism Spears received about a concert performance. Crocker maintains that his theatrics were genuine and not a performance. Whatever the case, his engagement, willingness to display raw emotion, and comfort with his femininity gained him thousands of fans and haters alike.

**•••Shoot•••**

- ✦ Put on a show. Let the kid in you loose.
- ✦ Sing, dance, tell a joke, tell a story or create a character. With your work from prior weeks in mind, shoot a video with only one goal: that it be entertaining however you define it.

**Process Pieces:**

*...we're going to look back at many facets of old media and realize that we were living in a desert disguised as a rain forest.*

**—Steven Johnson**

Do you have an activity coming up that has a beginning, middle and end? For example, one man video blogged about the process of setting up an organic garden in his back yard. Not only did his viewers benefit by learning from his mistakes, but he remained motivated to push ahead and complete his project. Finishing the project becomes more likely with viewers from around the world cheering your progress. In this scenario, everyone wins.

**•••Shoot•••**

Choose something that you know how to do well and video it. Maybe you have perfected a favorite recipe, can fix a bicycle with ease, or know a cool Photoshop trick? Whatever it is, break it down into steps and record it.

- ✦ Explain each step clearly and don't assume too much prior knowledge.

- ✦ Make your demonstration as visual as you can.

- ✦ Pay attention to the things that *you* learn while you explain it. Explaining something forces us to see it with "beginner's eyes." New ideas often arise because of this.

**Connect:**

Posting video online can foster conversations and connections with others across the world. Johnnydurham19 is a British video blogger who attempts to engage with his viewers. In one video blog he references the fact that he has about 25,000 viewers. "This is more people than I personally know," he says. "So let's get to know each other." He then encourages people to introduce themselves through video responses.

Another creative video blogger is Mary Matthews. She created a video called the *Slow Dramatic Clap of the Internet*. The video spoofs a cliché of several films from the 1980s. Someone starts clapping slowly but confidently. Others hesitate, but then a few join in. Soon the entire room or stadium, etc., is clapping. Mary asked individuals to submit their own interpretation of the long clap and then edited them together to entertaining and rousing effect.

*When we try to pick out anything by itself, we find it hitched to everything else in the Universe.*

**—John Muir**

In a similar vein, *Eternal Moonwalk* includes an often hilarious and hypnotic sequence of people from around the world "moonwalking" one after the other in their own unique ways.

## —Get Your 15-Minutes...If You Want 'Em—

Cultural theorists often connect fame and celebrity to the "rise of the visual" in our society. Or you could say we're becoming more and more like peacocks. And in the age of social media, strutting our tail feathers is easier than ever.

Fame is no longer a top-down occurrence. It leaps from the sides, the bottom, and all around. It could happen to anyone. It could happen to you. Because of this, some people seek a secret online fame formula. It's as if fame could be purchased in a kit and by following the recipe one morning we'll be adored by millions before dinner.

Assuming you want to open the Pandora's box of fame, suggestions that make sense tend to come from a marketing perspective. For example in Frederick Levy's book *15 Minutes of Fame,* the author recommends that in order to stand out online users should:

- → Make short, unique videos.
- → Create video responses to other more popular YouTubers.
- → Choose broad topics *(my advice is to choose topics you have passion for).*
- → Make collaborative videos *(with other more popular users).*
- → Make videos that directly comment on current YouTube culture.

*Fame is becoming ours; we are making it ours, as we are doing so much else in our culture. Fame now reflects us.*

**—David Weinberger**

But pursuing the marketing angle before taking the time to explore using video to mine your own emotional terrain would be a mistake in my opinion. Fame is most likely to be stumbled upon by expressing what is actually unique to you, not what you think is unique based on marketing analysis. Micro-celebrities such as Brookers or Gary Brolsma didn't set out to be famous—it just happened. No matter what you do, there are no guarantees, so you might as well enjoy yourself and express something authentic.

People seek fame for many different reasons. Some want to promote a product or their business, others want to be heard or share their talents and still others want to make a difference. Sometimes there is also the deeper reason of wanting to be loved. We *all* want to be loved. It's part of being human. However, fame seldom provides love. There are numerous mainstream examples of celebrity where fame has destroyed lives—Michael Jackson, Elvis Presley, and Marilyn Monroe to name three. On the other hand, there are many more famous people who enjoy their fame and even use it to benefit others.

There's nothing wrong with wanting recognition, but many people want more than recognition—they want Fame with a capital "F" but can't define why. They just know that life will be somehow better once they have it.

I can't speak from experience, and it's not for anyone but you to decide whether fame is pursued. If fame calls to you, there's nothing wrong in pursuing it. But be clear why you're pursuing it and what you expect will change once you get some. Fame is an extraordinarily powerful force in our culture. It only makes sense to pause for a minute if we are "bitten by the bug" to look and see what actually bit us.

### •••Shoot•••

*In some ways YouTube fame brings all of the negative sides of stardom without the money and the perks.*

**—Kevin Nalts**

✦ Make a one-minute entry about a time when you felt appreciated, for example: performing or making a speech, public acknowledgment for a job well done, or even a birthday or wedding celebration. What feelings arose?

✦ Make a one-minute entry talking about why you would (or would not) like to become famous.

✦ You are now as famous as you hope to be. Someone asks you in an interview, "How has your life changed?"

### ▲Replay▲

❖ What thoughts occur when you hear yourself expressing your reasons for or against fame? Is there anything you've left unsaid?

❖ If you stated positive life changes due to fame, are there ways to manifest them that aren't contingent on becoming famous? Fame might happen tomorrow or it could be a long wait. Make an entry about these or put them into action so that you win either way.

## —That's a Wrap!—

This brings us to the official end of the *Eight-Week Workshop*, but it's not really an end at all. You've shot a lot of video over the past weeks. Take some time to look back at your footage. Pay attention to the exercises that affected you the most. Use these as guideposts going forward. Feel free to keep using these exercises in what I hope becomes a daily video practice for you. Most importantly, experiment on your own.

- → What stands out to you as remarkable?
- → Did issues arise that warrant additional exploration?
- → Which exercises did you like the most? Dislike the most? Why?
- → What effect has video had (or not had) on everyday life?
- → What inspiration do you have for your own further entries or projects?

*The world is round and the place which may seem like the end may also be only the beginning.*

**—Ivy Baker Priest**

If you're like most people, you've had your own ideas for using video in the past weeks. Maybe you also found yourself disagreeing with or resisting some exercises. Try to understand what didn't speak to you and use that energy to create something that does. It's guaranteed that if you create something that ignites a spark in you, it will also inspire others if that's your goal. Either way, it's a great way to further define a video journaling or blogging process that's uniquely yours.

In the next section, we'll look at the magic of editing. Then we'll explore an often overlooked, but essential, topic: archiving your videos so that with any luck they will last the rest of your life and well beyond...perhaps even one billion years.

# Part Four

## Cut!—
## Putting It All Together

# 11

# To Edit or Not to Edit

In the not too distant future, video editing may become as widely used and as accessible as word processing is today. Editing is a powerful tool that can be used to creatively shape your material in nearly infinite ways. In simple terms, editing means that you select which parts of your videos to include or exclude in the final piece. Choosing whether to edit your video is partly the result of the time you have to spend and what your end goals are.

When reading overly wordy text, it's easy to scan through for the good bits. It's more difficult when watching a rambling video. On a basic level, you can cut out segments to make your video more concise ("umms" and "errs" for example) or change the meaning altogether by rearranging your sentence order. You can also add meaningful elements such as photos or other videos, text, graphics, voiceovers, and music.

> Editing can shape your material in nearly infinite ways.

Following are further reasons to edit.

- → You want to create a video blog. Going public often benefits from editing, even if it's basic. You might also edit out parts of your entry that you want to keep private.
- → If your goal is the highest number of views, shorter is better. If you watch many of the more popular videos online, they are short and often edit out all the "umms," "errs," and pauses.
- → This has led to an energetic (some might say frenetic) editing style that is ubiquitous on the Net. The standard video blog entry tends to run from one or two minutes or up to five minutes on

the long side. Longer pieces tend to have been edited to improve the flow and keep people watching.

→ If you want to select pieces from several different video entries, you'll need to edit. For example, you might choose entries you've made on a certain theme and splice them together.

→ Anything imaginable—if it can be turned into digital form—can be added to your video journal or blog. For example:

- Either scan or take digital photos of your artwork and include them in your piece.
- Include digital photographs or videos that others have shared with you.
- Scan portions of your paper journal (if you keep one) and intersperse it with your video entry.
- Add text or graphics to your piece to highlight an emotion or layer it with a new one. For example, editorialize your own entry with text as to what is *really* going on now that you look back at it.
- Add external sound, music, and sound effects or make an additional voiceover on top of what you already recorded.

*But I suppose film is distinctive because of its nature, of its being able to cut through time with editing.*

**—Oliver Stone**

Simple editing can now be done online. For example, Kaltura is an open source (it is free of charge to use) video editor specifically created for online content. Newer mobile phones have simple editing software built in.

In a pinch, YouTube has a function that allows users to add text (think "thought bubbles"). It's common to see video bloggers include text that reads something like "what I meant to say was <BLANK>" rather than editing the line out.

Remember, in many ways editing is the video version of word processing, so let your imagination take over. The possibilities are endless.

## —Video Editing Software—

If you own a computer manufactured in the past few years it already includes basic editing software as part of the operating system (Windows or Apple). This basic software allows you to edit your video and even add simple text titles and effects.

The basic concept common to all video editing software is the timeline. The timeline is the linear area where you add footage and subsequently rearrange it. This is done by either clicking and dragging the clips to a different place on the timeline or using various other tools unique to the software.

### Apple iMovie:

*Film editing is now something almost everyone can do at a simple level and enjoy it, but to take it to a higher level requires the same dedication and persistence that any art form does.*

**—Walter Murch**

If you use an Apple computer, then you probably already have some version of iMovie. iMovie is part of Apple's iLife suite that also includes tools such as Garage Band (for creating music from loops), iTunes and iDVD. If you don't have iMovie on your computer, you can purchase it as part of the iLife suite.

### Windows Movie Maker:

Not wanting to be outdone by Apple, Microsoft includes its own, free video editing software as part of the Windows platform. Movie Maker offers all the basics that iMovie does but in a different format. The new version of Windows Movie Maker is now called Windows Live Movie Maker with some changes in features.

### Pro Software:

If you're planning a more sophisticated project, there are several other applications that are excellent. Professional software gives increased options for organizing material and a wider range of tools with which to manipulate your video footage.

For the Macintosh, Final Cut Pro is an excellent choice. Used by many pro editors and independent filmmakers, it offers a streamlined workflow and options to do just about anything you might need. For Windows, consider Adobe Premiere Pro or Sony Vegas.

## —Creating a Larger Project—

Many people begin a video journal without any set goal in mind but discover a destination begins to take shape as the process becomes a daily habit. Certain themes emerge. These themes might inspire a larger project. The project could evolve into something that you exhibit publicly such as some form of documentary, or it could be purely for your own journey (or to share with close friends and family).

Once you've identified a theme or topic, the next step is to determine how much material you have already videoed that applies and how much new material you'd like to shoot. Perhaps you've discovered that one emerging theme is a wry sense of humor regarding the evolving environmental challenges we face. Or you might make a piece about a person you are close to, a major event in your life, or an entirely experimental piece such as a "mash-up" of several of your past entries combined with clips you've found on the Internet.

*Creativity involves breaking out of established patterns in order to look at things in a different way.*

**—Edward de Bono**

Return to your past entries and gather every instance that relates to your theme. Once you determine what other material you need, begin shooting or gather it from other sources.

Collect all of your footage into your editing program and organize it in a way that makes sense to you. This may mean laying it out chronologically at first so you have a broad overview. Having done this, you might find that the chronological order isn't the most effective, in which case you can change the order again.

That's the beauty of editing—juxtaposing your video entries to create an entirely new level of meaning. Experiment with different shot orders. Pay attention to the way each arrangement affects you on an emotional level. Try to see your material with "beginner's eyes." In other words, look at it as if for the first time. When we have lived something, it's easy to become trapped in the chronology of that event.

This is your chance to break free from what actually happened and create something entirely new. Ask yourself: What if this one thing had happened before or after the other? Or perhaps not at all.

One general strategy for efficient editing of a personal project is to start early. Don't wait until you have countless hours of footage. Begin when you have a small amount and the footage content is still fresh in mind. Edit as you go. You can then rearrange and reorganize again when you've finished shooting.

You can find further resources for learning about editing at www.nakedlensbook.com.

*As human beings, our greatness lies not so much in being able to remake the world—that is the myth of the atomic age—as in being able to remake ourselves.*

**—Gandhi**

# 12

# Video Blogging for Cash

A sizeable number of people have been able to parlay their video blogging experiments into well paying careers. Many others make a bit of extra money every month and have fun doing it.

Corey Williams, aka "Mr. Safety" rose to popularity with his *Mean Kitty Song*—a humorous, homemade music video about his cat, Sparta. Other creative videos followed and, according to a recent *New York Times* article, Williams now averages $17,000 to $20,000 per month using the YouTube revenue sharing program, product placement, and sponsorships.[1]

> What are your passions?

Revenue sharing programs place small ads at the bottom of your videos. Revenue gained from these ads is split between the host site and the video creator. In the case of YouTube, users need to apply to their Partnership Program, and acceptance is based on the popularity of the user's videos. Other sites such as metacafe and revver have no application. You'll receive a fee per every thousand viewers or so. This can mount up if the video is popular. If you have marketing savvy like Corey Williams or Lucas Cruikshank (creator of Fred Figglehorn, who has paid for his college education many times over) you can also find companies interested in sponsoring your work. Cruikshank even managed to land a feature film based on his Fred character.

Another way video creators make extra money is to start a regular video blog that includes affiliate advertising. Wordpress offers various plug-ins that help you set up video on your site. If you've surfed the Net, you've definitely seen affiliate ads. They are the small text-based links (though they can also be banners) that you find on blog pages and websites targeted toward the subject matter of the site. In simple terms, each time someone clicks on your link, you receive a small amount of money. Affiliate ads can be provided by Google or individual agreements can be made with websites where a percentage of each sale is provided to the referring website (in this case you) in addition to the clicks.

There are numerous other methods video bloggers have used to make money, and sometimes a sizeable amount. Video bloggers have:

- → Used their video blogs to expand small businesses.
- → Created products related to their video blog.
- → Sold their video blogs to larger media companies.
- → Been offered their own TV shows.
- → Consulted and taught video blogging to others.

*The best part of all this isn't the business or the brand building or the opportunity...they all fail in comparison to the fact that we are able to meet so many darn people!*

**—Gary Vaynerchuk**

The most important thing is to consider what your interests are. What are your passions? Gary Vaynerchuk, turned his love of fine wine into dollars when he started *Wine Library TV* and built his family's small wine business into a national player. He also received book deals and TV offers, all because his video blogging efforts transformed him from a local presence to a global presence. This takes hard work, skill, and a bit of luck too, but new opportunities are available that weren't just a few years back.

There also may be overlooked ways that video might apply to your current job or business. If you deal with customers or clients from a distance, how might video be used to connect with them more intimately? Completing the workshop in this book puts you ahead from the beginning. There are many derivative video blogs, but those that are innovative are much more likely to find their own audience. Once you've started to build a following, you may need to give things a little push by learning some social networking skills. Several websites and books on video blogging and Internet marketing are listed at www.nakedlensbook.com.

For now, the money that flows to individuals is still a mere trickle compared to what the giant media companies control. It also tends to follow the familiar corporate sponsor pattern. With the trend moving away from big business and the rising popularity of various community-based alternative currencies such as BerkShares in Massachusetts, it will be interesting to see what new, more equitable opportunities are invented in the future.

13

# Plan for the Future

Paper journals exist that have survived for hundreds of years. Hidden in dusty attics and stashed in musty basements, they've endured scorching summers and frigid winters and somehow survived. They may be a bit damaged here or there, but generally they are legible. Force a collection of videotapes, DVDs, or a computer hard drive to suffer the same harsh conditions, and they will be decimated in far less time.

The durability of the material is key. For example, I produced a documentary that used archival video from the 1970s and 1980s. The 1970s had plenty of usable material available because film was still in use during that period. Film is a much more durable format than video. In the 1980s the transition from film to video occurred. Not only is video less hardy, but there were also compatibility issues as old video equipment had become obsolete. Footage from the 1980s was ironically much more difficult to obtain, though it is more recent history.

> Archiving isn't exactly a party topic so people don't give it much thought.

Even with the best care possible, digital information is challenging to store long-term. If your goal is to keep your video around for five or ten years, then you shouldn't have any major difficulties. But if you want to keep your video material as a record for your children, grandchildren, or perhaps even generations far in the future, then you'll need to start thinking about archiving.

Archiving is a complex topic. Professional archivists make their living consulting with institutions on how to preserve material. They oversee and manage vast libraries to make sure they are maintained correctly. It's not only a matter of physical integrity; it's a matter of future compatibility.

Remember VHS-C? If you don't, you aren't in the minority. It was a small-format VHS tape that was popular in the mid to late 1990s. No one manufactures VHS-C decks or cameras today to my knowledge. If you needed one, perhaps you could find used equipment on eBay—but as the years pass and equipment fails without being remanufactured, this will become increasingly challenging. If and when you do find one, the price will likely be high. Probably far more than the original price!

Another recent example is VHS vs. Betamax. Depending on how old you are, you may not remember Betamax. If you're even younger, VHS might seem archaic. All of these old analog formats have died or are in the process of dying out. If you keep footage in these formats, I highly recommend you transfer them to digital. Speaking of digital, you might think that by shooting directly onto your computer hard drive or memory chip, you're immune from all of the above issues. This is true to a certain extent with some important caveats to follow.

*The camera is no more an instrument of preservation, the image is.*

**—Berenice Abbott**

### Hard Drives:

Hard drives can store a large quantity of material and are quite cheap. However, they are prone to being affected by dust and the passage of time. They can have catastrophic failures that render all the information inaccessible if the directory structure is damaged. That said, when managed properly they can be a good solution.

### Solid-State Storage:

Solid-state storage (storage on microchips such as USB drives) is quite durable but still too expensive to store large volumes of video content effectively. Prices keep falling though, and this is great news for archiving.

### DVDs/Blu-ray Disks:

Regular DVDs don't hold very much information (they range from 4 to 8 gigabytes), but they can be an option as well. They have an estimated life ranging from five to forty years depending on who you talk to. A Blu-ray disk holds about fifty gigabytes of information per disk currently and may be a viable option for you. It requires a special Blu-ray burner, and they haven't been around long enough to know for certain how long they will last.

## —Recommended Storage Strategies—

If this sounds discouraging, take heart. It's not as bad as it sounds. Archiving isn't exactly a party topic, so most people don't give it much, if any, thought. Even having awareness of the issue increases the likelihood that you'll be able to retain your material for a long time.

Unless you are the kind of person who loves to be the first to adopt a new technology, stick with one primary digital storage solution, keep two copies of your most important material and re-evaluate your options every four or five years.

*The best way to predict the future is to invent it.*
**—Alan Kay**

For example, if you decide to store your video on hard drives, five years from now look into what new storage technologies might exist. Perhaps solid-state chip memory will be affordable enough to use instead of hard disks. Or there may be a "super" Blu-ray disk that records ten times what a current Blu-ray disk holds.

For now, choose one strategy from the following and put it out of your mind. It will drive you nuts otherwise, and you'd be better off putting your energy into your video blogs and journals.

### DV/HDV Tapes:

The oldest DV tapes I own go back over twelve years. So far, there hasn't been any noticeable problem with them. To be on the safe side, DV tapes should be "cloned" which means rerecording and making a DV duplicate of each tape every five years or so. Alternatively, you could consider backing the tapes up to a hard drive and storing the tapes separately. The data on HDV tapes is more highly compressed though, so they may not last as long.

### Hard Drives:

For most people with limited time and money, storing material on removable hard drives makes the most sense. If you're shooting in a compressed format such as a webcam, mobile phone, or palm-sized camcorder utilizes, you'll be able to store hundreds of hours of footage on one hard drive.

Remember that you should back up the hard drives regularly whether to DVD or to another hard drive. If you store all your material on one drive, you're asking for heartache should the drive fail. Keep your backups in a separate location. This could mean a separate room or a different location altogether, depending on your circumstances and level of caution.

### Online Storage:

If you choose to upload your material, provided that the service stays in business (and doesn't change its terms and conditions and delete your material), you will have another backup though it likely will be reduced quality. No one foresees YouTube or Google hitting financial problems or running out of storage in the next several years—but who knows what will happen in ten or more years?

*A photograph can be an instant of life captured for eternity that will never cease looking back at you.*

**—Brigitte Bardot**

## —The Long Range View—

If you regularly back up your hard drives and migrate your material to newer formats over the next five or ten years, then there's no reason your material shouldn't last for your lifetime and beyond. Storage technology is developing at a rapid rate. There's a good chance that in ten years or perhaps much sooner, a better solution will come along.

Researchers at the University of California at Berkeley have discovered a promising storage technology that uses carbon nanotubes. The technology would hold roughly twenty-five DVDs' worth of info in a postage stamp device and have a theoretical life span of about ONE BILLION years.[1] One billion years ago, multicellular organisms were about the only thing going and dinosaurs wouldn't appear for roughly seven hundred million more. It's safe to say that if this technology holds up to its promise, there will be much bigger questions we'll face during that time frame.

# 14

# Video Healing & Support

People often use written journaling either to supplement ongoing therapy or as a type of self-therapy, and video journaling may be able to fulfill a similar role. Video blogging is also frequently used as a way of finding support and community.

> Whatever your goals, it's essential that everyone in the group is clear about them.

Adrian Sudbury, a twenty-seven-year-old British man diagnosed with Leukemia, started *Baldy's Blog*. Using both video and text, Adrian bravely shared his journey with the world, from the first days of coping with his diagnosis, to chemotherapy, and ultimately deciding not to pursue further treatment. With only a few months to live, he spent his final time lobbying for bone marrow donation awareness through his text and video blogs. Any difficult or traumatic passage in life could conceivably be shared with the hope of receiving support and benefiting others in the process.

When Brian Nessel (bnessel1973 on YouTube) lost his son to SIDS, video blogging became a form of therapy. He expressed aspects of himself on YouTube that he couldn't release otherwise and found support. In his own words "this community helped bring me life again and there's something really special in that."

## —Video Therapy—

If you already see a therapist or plan on doing so, consider integrating your video journaling practice. Family therapists in particular have been able to successfully integrate video into their work.

One therapist I'm familiar with reports that she videos her patients and then gives them the recording to review for homework. She offers the example of a situation where a couple argues vehemently, neither one really hearing what the other says. Once they've calmed down at home, they can listen to what the other person is saying. This can allow for healing to occur outside therapy, ultimately lowering costs.

If you can't find a therapist interested in using video during your session, you could instead video journal after therapy to keep track of your progress. Or consider bringing in one of your entries to talk about with your therapist. It may not be necessary to physically bring in the recording. Just using an entry to spark a new thought or feeling to explore can be enough.

## —Video Support Group—

Forming a group is another way to receive support and feedback on an informal basis. If you are considering whether you want to start video blogging, screening your entries for a group first is also an excellent way to test the waters.

If your focus is on creating video blogs, you can set timelines for when videos should be ready to post as well as provide feedback and direction. A group also allows you to share pieces of your video work and trade tips with others who have the same goals.

*Some people say YouTube videos should be made to help change the world. I've made mine to help me live in it.*

**—Brian Nessel**

### Forming an In-Person Group:

Groups of three to seven people are ideal. Larger groups can work, but organization becomes challenging when it comes to viewing videos and making sure everyone has their needs met. If you have less than three, then there's no reason why two people can't get together to support one another but you'll lose out on the group dynamic. Try meetup.com if there aren't enough people you know personally.

### Forming an Online Group:

Actual physical meetings aren't required to form a group. You can use online video instead. Video chats and group experiments can be organized and tried out. You can upload your videos and receive feedback, tips, and support all from the comfort of your own home. Online groups can generally be larger than in-person groups without suffering from organizational challenges. Several online groups of various kinds are listed at www.nakedlensbook.com.

## —Sharing Private Work—

Sharing private video journals deserves a special mention. Be clear if there is specific feedback that you are (or are not) looking for. For example, you might be using video to help grow and work through a difficult time in your life. If this is your goal, you'll be looking to the group to provide you with some non-judgmental support but probably won't be looking for critique of your on-camera aesthetic.

Whatever your goals, it's essential that everyone in the group is clear about them. This is important as a long-term consideration for the group and for your specific needs because goals will shift over time. Following are some ground rules to consider:

> *You must trust and believe in people or life becomes impossible.*
>
> **—Anton Chekhov**

1. Screen what feels appropriate for you. If nothing fits, talk about your experience rather than showing material. Don't reveal yourself before you're ready.
2. Let your video speak for itself. Don't defend it or make excuses. Screening a video is like a mini "birthing," but once the video is there for the group to see, it can do fine on its own.
3. Maintain the confidentiality of your fellow group members. This allows the safety necessary for people to relax.
4. Aim for mutual support rather than criticism.
5. If someone is having a rough time, show that you care and support them without trying to fix things. The motivation behind the group should be one of shared presence, not group therapy.
6. Maintain a sense of humor. Think of the group as a lab for experimentation where you can have fun. Make as many mistakes as you can and encourage others in the group to do the same.

# 15

# Where to From Here?

Years ago I decided to sell the shiny new DV camcorder I had bought back in 1996, which was no longer new and no longer shiny. I needed to purchase updated equipment with better quality to shoot for broadcast. I carefully laid my faithful camera and its accessories out on my coffee table in preparation for the craigslist rendezvous. I remember thinking back to the many adventures we had shared over the years.

My mobile phone interrupted my sentimental reverie—the potential buyer was downstairs. I was still in my Midtown Manhattan apartment at the time. In addition to its lack of a kitchen, the apartment was also missing a door buzzer, so I traipsed down the three flights to let the guy in.

> The video camera has proven itself mightier than the tank.

Walking back up the stairs, a sudden thought occurred to me. "Keep it." I didn't want to sell the camera after all. This was despite the fact that I absolutely required the money to put toward my expensive new equipment. Was it too late to tell the guy that I had changed my mind?

After all, that little camera had travelled all over the continent with me. She had survived the dust of the Nevada desert at Burning Man and the bone-rattling cold of a central Canadian Christmas. She had recorded my first serious relationship in New York and my tears over its ending. She had patiently listened to me and, except for the occasional cleaning, never once pretended to be broken or sick. A lot of the light that passed through my eyes, the experiences, the places, the people I cared for, had also passed through her lens.

Thinking all of these things, I realized something. I realized that I needed to sell that little camera, and sell her quick. And so I did.

Because this book focuses on video journaling and blogging, there has naturally been major emphasis on using your video camera. Yet of course, just as the pen isn't the writing, neither is the video camera anything other than a tool, one way to channel thoughts, work through emotions, and communicate ideas.

What sometimes gets lost when speaking about video technology is the broader picture. Nearly one billion people entered the 21st century lacking the ability to read or write their name, let alone start a video blog.[1] And many in the developing world don't have Internet access. However, there are signs that this is changing.

In India, the *Goan People's Film Festival* offered a workshop on video blogging, mobile phones, and citizen journalism to help confront issues of globalization.[2] Though the developing world lacks computer access, they aren't far behind with mobile phone usage. Mobile phones can now function as highly capable media production and distribution tools.

In Brazil, the *Earth Video Blogging Project* empowered communities and underlined the importance of allowing local culture to shape technology rather than it be imposed from outside.[3] Media has historically been dominated by a Western mind-set. Now that this is hopefully changing, new perspectives will enrich media's evolution.

*Where the spirit does not work with the hand there is no art.*

**—Leonardo da Vinci**

However, perhaps video won't reach its full potential until it dissolves into the fabric of everyday life and we take it for granted, much as we take pens and word processors for granted today. According to UCSD Visual Studies professor Lev Manovich, it's only a matter of time before *constantly* broadcasting our lives becomes as common as email.[4] Lending credence to this, Microsoft is set to license their SenseCam technology that allows users to wear a continually recording miniature camera around their necks.[5] Some such cameras include GPS, motion sensors and temperature monitoring. So called "life blogging," currently a fringe interest, may enter the mainstream.[6]

What would a world like this look like? I suggest that whether or not this happens is not what's crucial. What is crucial is that our emotional and spiritual life remains part of the equation.

Using history as an example, one key component to the above may be engagement. In the past, mass social change occurred through the medium of text—for example, Martin Luther and the Protestant reformation or the Declaration of Human Rights. Now video leads the way. Think Tiananmen Square, Rodney King, Oscar Grant, or the Iranian election protests. The video camera is proving itself mightier than the tank.

Video is not "the" solution to our problems, whether personal or global. Yet now is the time to keep pushing the limits of what it *can* do. Everyone who picks up a camera holds this potential in her or his own hands. We don't need to wait for "them" to decide, because we are part of the conversation. On a mass level, this not only has the potential to change society—it radically changes the *way* that we change. Video cameras may be nothing more than boxes that capture light and sound, but for the first time in history, millions can capture their own light and brighten the world.

*The big question is whether you are going to be able to say a hearty yes to your adventure.*
**—Joseph Campbell**

Actively using video, demystifying it, feeling its texture and slipping beneath its hard technological shell to its core—the deeply human desire for contact—is an integral part of the process. Video journaling or video blogging may not be the only way to do this, but it is a powerful one. When we reclaim video as our own and use it mindfully, engagement can't help but be present because *we* are present.

## Notes


### Chapter 1: Introduction

1. Jakob Nielsen, PhD, 10/02/2009, <http://www.90-9-1.com/>.

### Chapter 3: The Power of Journaling

1. Rainer, Tristine. 1978. *The new diary : How to use a journal for self-guidance and expanded creativity.* Los Angeles; New York: J. P. Tarcher; distributed by St. Martin's Press.

2. Baikie, Karen A., and Kay Wilhelm. "Emotional and Physical Health Benefits of Expressive Writing." *Adv Psychiatr Treat* 11.5 (2005): 338-46.

3. Pennebaker, J. W., Kiecolt-Glaser, J. K., & Glaser, R. (1988). "Disclosure of traumas and immune function: Health implications for psychotherapy." *Journal of Consulting and Clinical Psychology*, Vol. 56, pp. 239-245.

4.Ko, H-C. & Kuo, F-Y. (2009). "Can blogging enhance subjective well-being through self-disclosure?" *CyberPsychology & Behavior*, 12(1), 75-79. DOI 10.1089/cpb.2008.0163

5. Pennebaker, James W. 1997. *Opening up : The healing power of expressing emotions.* New York: Guildford Press.

6. Esterling, Brian A.; Antoni, Michael H.; Fletcher, Mary Ann; Margulies, Scott; Schneiderman, Neil. "Emotional disclosure through writing or speaking modulates latent Epstein-Barr virus antibody titers." Journal of Consulting and Clinical Psychology. Vol 62(1), Feb 1994, 130-140.

7. Parr, Clare J., and Sam Cartwright-Hatton. 2009. "Social anxiety in adolescents: The effect of video feedback on anxiety and the self-evaluation of performance." *Clinical Psychology & Psychotherapy* 16, (1): 46-54.

8. Rodebaugh, Thomas L., and Dianne L. Chambless. 2002. "The effects of video feedback on self-perception of performance: A replication and extension." *Cognitive Therapy and Research* 26, (5) (10/01): 629-44.

9. 10/24/2009 <http://www.barnard.edu/sfonline/blogs/printpla.htm>.

### Chapter 4: Why Be On-Camera?

1. Harley, Dave, and Geraldine Fitzpatrick. 2009. "Creating a conversational context through video blogging: A case study of Geriatric1927." *Comput.Hum.Behav.* 25, (3): 679-89.

2. Rotman, Dana, Jennifer Golbeck, and Jennifer Preece. 2009. "The community is where the rapport is —on sense and structure in the YouTube community." *Proceedings of the fourth international conference on Communities and technologies*, University Park, PA, USA.

3."*Forecast: The Next Decade of Video Technology* | People of the Screen." 10/24/2009 <http://peopleofthescreen.org/content/forecast-medium-making>.

4. "Blogtalk Downunder » *Media Rich versus Rich Media* (long single version)." 10/24/2009 <http://incsub.org/blogtalk/?page_id=76>.

### Chapter 5: The Road That Brought Us Here

1. Thoreau, Henry David, and Bradford Torrey. 1962. *The Journal of Henry D. Thoreau, Vol. 2.*, Dover Publications, p. xx.

2. Mostow, Joshua S. 2004. *At the house of gathered leaves : Shorter biographical and autobiographical narratives from Japanese court literature.* Honolulu: University of Hawaiì Press, pp. 35-38.

3. "Centenary College: Women Writers." 10/24/2009 <http://www.centenarycollege.edu/cms/en/student-writing-website/link-one/essay/anais-nin-revisited/>.

4. Rugg, Linda Haverty. "Keaton's Leap: Self-Projection and Autobiography in Film" *Biography* - Volume 29, Number 1, Winter 2006, pp. v-xiii

5. "Weathered underground - Features - Film - *Time Out New York.*" 11/4/2009 <http://www.timeout.com/film/newyork/features/show-feature/3313/weathered-underground.html>.

6. Smith, Roberta. (1993). "UP AND COMING: Sadie Benning; A Video Artist Who Talks Through a Keyhole." *The New York Times* March 28, 1993.

7. "Numa Numa - Wikipedia, the free encyclopedia." 10/24/2009 <http://en.wikipedia.org/wiki/Numa_Numa>.

8. "YouTube serves up 100 million videos a day online - USATODAY.com." 10/26/2009 <http://www.usatoday.com/tech/news/2006-07-16-youtube-views_x.htm>.

9. "YouTube - YouTube Fact Sheet." 10/20/2009 <http://www.youtube.com/t/fact_sheet>.

**Chapter 10: Week One**

1. Hollingworth, Harry L. *The Psychology of the Audience.* New York, Cincinnati etc.: American Book Company, 1935.

2. Wolpe, Joseph. 1968. "Psychotherapy by reciprocal inhibition." *Integrative Psychological and Behavioral Science* 3, (4) (10/01): 234-40.

**Chapter 10: Week Two**

1. Though my interpretation is slightly different, it was Tristine Rainer's book, *The New Diary* that inspired me to look at Fellini's film, *8 1/2* from this perspective.

2. "The Funniest Thing About This Video..." http://www.youtube.com/watch?v=YZnLhsWoWHE

3. Ozdemir E., Norton A., Schlaug G. "Shared and distinct neural correlates of singing and speaking" (2006) *NeuroImage*, 33 (2), pp. 628-635.

4. "When Diary Pages Can Fill Out Lives." *New York Times* 16 October, 1991, sec. C, . 10

5. "Cooley - The Work - Looking Glass Self." 10/24/2009 <http://web.archive.org/web/20070814013608/www2.pfeiffer.edu/~lridener/DSS/Cooley/COOLWRK.HTML>.

**Chapter 10: Week Three**

1. Epel, Elissa, et al. "Can Meditation Slow Rate of Cellular Aging? Cognitive Stress, Mindfulness, and Telomeres." *Annals of the New York Academy of Sciences* 1172.Longevity, Regeneration, and Optimal Health Integrating Eastern and Western Perspectives (2009): 34-53.

2. Brown, Kirk Warren, and Richard M. Ryan. 2003. "The benefits of being present: Mindfulness and its role in psychological well-being." *Journal of Personality and Social Psychology* 84, (4): 822-48. Kabat-Zinn, Jon. *Wherever You Go, there You are : Mindfulness Meditation in Everyday Life.* New York: Hyperion, 2005. Davidson, Richard J., et al. "Alterations in Brain and Immune Function Produced by Mindfulness Meditation." *Psychosom Med* 65.4 (2003): 564-70. O. Mason, and Hargreaves I. "A Qualitative Study of Mindfulness-Based Cognitive Therapy for Depression." *British Journal of Medical Psychology* 74 (1 June 2001): 197,212(16). Horan, Roy. 2009. "The neuropsychological connection between creativity and meditation." *Creativity Research Journal* 21, (2): 199. Barnes S, Brown KW, Krusemark E, Campbell WK, Rogge RD. "The Role of Mindfulness in Romantic Relationship Satisfaction and Responses to Relationship Stress." *Journal of Marital and Family Therapy*, October 2007.

3. Hanh, Nhat 1991. *Peace is every step : The path of mindfulness in everyday life.* New York, N.Y.: Bantam Books.

4. Williams, Redford B., and Virginia Parrott Williams. 1994; 1993. *Anger kills : Seventeen strategies for controlling the hostility that can harm your health*. 1 HarperPerennial ed. New York: HarperCollins Publishers.

5. Bushman, Brad J. "Does Venting Anger Feed Or Extinguish the Flame? Catharsis, Rumination, Distraction, Anger, and Aggressive Responding." *Pers Soc Psychol Bull* 28.6 (2002): 724-31.

**Chapter 10: Week Four**

1. Luers, W. 2007. "Cinema Without Show Business: A Poetics of Vlogging." Post Identity, 5(1), http://hdl.handle.net/2027/spo.pid9999.0005.2105.

2. Kashdan, Todd B., Anjali Mishra, William E. Breen, and Jeffrey J. Froh. 2009. "Gender differences in gratitude: Examining appraisals, narratives, the willingness to express emotions, and changes in psychological needs." *Journal of Personality* 77, (3): 691-730.

3. Simmons, Annette. 2001. *The story factor : Secrets of influence from the art of storytelling.* New York: Basic Books.

**Chapter 10: Week Five**

1. Fullwood, Chris, and Gwyneth Doherty-Sneddon. 2006. "Effect of gazing at the camera during a video link on recall." *Applied Ergonomics* 37, (2) (3): 167-75.

**Chapter 10: Week Six**

1. history. Dictionary.com. Dictionary.com Unabridged. Random House, Inc. http://dictionary.reference.com/browse/history (accessed: January 7, 2010).

**Chapter 10: Week Seven**

1. Cameron, Julia. 1992. *The artist's way : A spiritual path to higher creativity. Inner workbook.* Los Angeles, CA: Jeremy P. Tarcher/Perigee.

2. Smith, C. 2006. "Where do you want to go today? Buddhism's role in bringing spirituality into the next generation of web technologies," discussion paper for the *Spirituality/Technology Dialogues: A Convergence of Ancient Wisdom and Modern Tools, Human Interface Technology Laboratory*, University of Washington.

**Chapter 10: Week Eight**

1. http://momentshowing.typepad.com/momentshowing/images/coffeeblog.mov

2. Mallon, Thomas. 1995; 1984. *A book of one's own : People and their diaries.* St. Paul, Minn.: Hungry Mind Press.

3. "Wesch - Anthropology Program at Kansas State University." 10/27/2009 <http://ksu-anth.weebly.com/wesch.html>.

4. Lange, Patricia G. 2007. "Publicly private and privately public: Social networking on YouTube." *Journal of Computer-Mediated Communication* 13, (1) (Oct): 361-80.

5. "Television." 10/27/2009 <http://www.csun.edu/science/health/docs/tv&health.html>.

6. http://www.srgnet.com/us/wp-content/uploads/2009/01/tv-video-hours-to-match-sleep-release-june-2008.pdf

7."Major News Stories Drive June Surge in U.S. Online Video Viewing to Record 157 Million Viewers - comScore, Inc." 10/23/2009 <http://www.comscore.com/Press_Events/Press_Releases/2009/8/Major_News_Stories_Drive_June_Surge_in_U.S._Online_Video_Viewing_to_Record_157_Million_Viewers>.

**Chapter 12: Video Blogging for Cash**

1. "YouTube Videos Pull In Real Money - NYTimes.com." 10/23/2009 <http://www.nytimes.com/2008/12/11/business/media/11youtube.html>.

**Chapter 13: Plan for the Future**

1. Begtrup, G. E., et al. "Nanoscale Reversible Mass Transport for Archival Memory." *Nano letters* 9.5 (2009): 1835-8.

**Chapter 15: Where to From Here?**

1. "Illiteracy—The Bad News and the Good | David Boaz | Cato Institute: Daily Commentary." 10/22/2009 <http://www.cato.org/pub_display.php?pub_id=5551>.

2. "Using cellphones to portray people's bitter struggle for survival." 10/23/2009 <http://www.digitaljournal.com/article/262849>.

3. Figueiredo, Marco A., Paola Prado, Mauro A. Camara, and Ana M. Albuquerque. 2009. "Empowering rural citizen journalism via web 2.0 technologies." Paper presented at *C&T 2009: Proceedings of the fourth international conference on Communities and technologies*, University Park, PA, USA.

4. Manovich, Lev. "The Practice of Everyday (Media) Life: From Mass Consumption to Mass Cultural Production?" *Critical Inquiry* 35.2 (2009): 319-31. (p. 325)

5. "SenseCam 2009 Home." 10/23/2009 <http://www.vicon.com/events/sensecam/home.htm>.

6. Millican, Tripp. 2005. "Iam: Experiences with persistent video recording, publishing and sharing." Paper presented at CARPE 2005: Proceedings of the 2nd *ACM workshop on Continuous archival and retrieval of personal experiences*, Hilton, Singapore.

## Sources *(Recommended Books in Bold)*


"Energy is Everything". [cited 10/20/2009 2009]. Available from http://www.geocities.com/davidwtalmage/quantum2.htm (accessed 10/20/2009).

"Watching the web watch me explorations of the domestic webcam." in *The Media in Transition Conference* Oct. 9, 1999 [database online].

**Adams, Kathleen. 1990. *Journal to the self : 22 paths to personal growth.* New York, NY: Warner Books.**

Baikie, Karen A., and Kay Wilhelm. 2005. "Emotional and physical health benefits of expressive writing." *Adv Psychiatr Treat 11*, (5): 338-46.

**Baldwin, Christina. 2007. *Life's companion : Journal writing as a spiritual practice.* Newly rev ed. New York: Bantam Books.**

Barlow, Janelle, Peta Peter, and Lewis Barlow. 2002. *Smart videoconferencing : New habits for virtual meetings.* 1st ed. San Francisco, Calif.: Berrett-Koehler.

Barry, Elizabeth. 2008. "Celebrity, cultural production and public life." *International Journal of Cultural Studies 11*, (3) (September 1): 251-8.

Benevenuto, Fabricio, Fernando Duarte, Tiago Rodrigues, Virgilio A. F. Almeida, Jussara M. Almeida, and Keith W. Ross. 2008. "Understanding video interactions in YouTube." Paper presented at MM 2008: *Proceeding of the 16th ACM international conference on Multimedia*, Vancouver, British Columbia, Canada.

Bourne, Edmund J. 2005. *The anxiety & phobia workbook.* 4th ed. Oakland, CA: New Harbinger Publications.

Bourne, Jennie, and Dave Burstein. 2009. *Web video : Making it great, getting it noticed.* Berkeley, CA: Peachpit Press.

Brown, Kirk Warren, and Richard M. Ryan. 2003. *The benefits of being present: Mindfulness and its role in psychological well-being.* 84, (4): 822-48.

Bryant, Stephanie Cottrell. 2006. *Videoblogging for dummies.* Hoboken, N.J.: Wiley.

**Cameron, Julia. 1992. *The artist's way : A spiritual path to higher creativity. Inner workbook.* Los Angeles, CA: Jeremy P. Tarcher/Perigee.**

Campbell, JoAnn. 1994. "Writing to heal: Using meditation in the writing process." *College Composition and Communication* 45, (2) (May): 246-51.

Carter, Mia. (1998). "The Politics of Pleasure: Cross-Cultural Autobiographic Performance in the Video Works of Sadie Benning." *Signs* Vol. 23, No. 3, *Feminisms and Youth Cultures* (Spring, 1998), The University of Chicago Press. pp. 745-769.

Cepero, Helen. 2008. *Journaling as a spiritual practice : Encountering God through attentive writing.* Downers Grove, Ill.: IVP Books.

Cha, Meeyoung, Haewoon Kwak, Pablo Rodriguez, Yong-Yeol Ahn, and Sue Moon. 2007. "I tube, you tube, everybody tubes: Analyzing the world's largest user generated content video system." Paper presented at *IMC 2007: Proceedings of the 7th ACM SIGCOMM conference on Internet measurement*, San Diego, California, USA.

Cook, David A. 1996. *A history of narrative film.* 3rd ed. New York: W.W. Norton.

**Csikszentmihalyi, Mihaly. 1990. *Flow : The psychology of optimal experience. 1st ed.* New York: Harper & Row.**

Dahlstrom, Lorraine M., and Pamela Espeland. 1990. *Writing down the days : 365 creative journaling ideas for young people.* Minneapolis, MN: Free Spirit Pub.

Decety, Jean, and Julie Grèzes. 2006. "The power of simulation: Imagining one's own and other's behavior." *Brain Research* 1079, (1) (3/24): 4-14.

**Dedman, Jay, and Joshua Paul. 2006. *Videoblogging.* Hoboken, NJ: Wiley.**

**Digh, Patti. 2009. *Life is a verb : 37 days to wake up, be mindful, and live intentionally.* Guilford, Conn.: Skirt.**

Epel, Elissa, Jennifer Daubenmier, Judith Tedlie Moskowitz, Susan Folkman, and Elizabeth Blackburn. 2009. "Can meditation slow rate of cellular aging? cognitive stress, mindfulness, and telomeres." *Annals of the New York Academy of Sciences* 1172, (Longevity, Regeneration, and Optimal Health Integrating Eastern and Western Perspectives): 34-53.

**Fahs, Chad. *How to do Everything with YouTube.* New York: McGraw-Hill, 2008.**

Falzone, Richard L., Sarah Hall, and Eugene V. Beresin. 2005. "How and why for the camera-shy: Using digital video in psychiatry." *Child and Adolescent Psychiatric Clinics of North America* 14, (3) (Jul): 603-12.

Fullwood, Chris, and Gwyneth Doherty-Sneddon. 2006. "Effect of gazing at the camera during a video link on recall." *Applied Ergonomics* 37, (2) (3): 167-75.

**Ganim, Barbara, and Susan Fox. 1999. *Visual journaling : Going deeper than words.* 1 Que ed. Wheaton, Ill.: Quest Books, Theosophical Pub. House.**

**Garfield, Steve. 2010. *Get Seen: Online Video Secrets to Building Your Business.* Hoboken, NJ: Wiley**

Goffman, Erving. 1971. *The presentation of self in everyday life.* A pelican book. Harmondsworth: Penguin.

Goldman, Ricki. 2004. "Video perspectivity meets wild and crazy teens: A design ethnography." *Cambridge Journal of Education* 34, (2) (Jun): 157-78.

Goldstein, Andrew M. 2006. "Vlog stars." *Rolling Stone*(999) (May 4): 26.

**Grason, Sandy. 2005. *Journalution : Journaling to awaken your inner voice, heal your life, and manifest your dreams.* Novato, Calif.: New World Library.**

Grimandi, Stefania. 2007. "Some reflections on the use of video recordings. commentary." *Infant Observation* 10, (1) (Apr): 89-90.

Harley, Dave, and Geraldine Fitzpatrick. 2009. "Creating a conversational context through video blogging: A case study of Geriatric1927." *Comput.Hum.Behav.* 25, (3): 679-89.

Harman, Willis W., and Howard Rheingold. 1984. *Higher creativity : Liberating the unconscious for breakthrough insights.* 1st ed. Los Angeles; Boston: J.P. Tarcher; Distributed by Houghton Mifflin.

Harvey, Allison G., David M. Clark, Anke Ehlers, and Ronald M. Rapee. 2000. "Social anxiety and self-impression: Cognitive preparation enhances the beneficial effects of video feedback following a stressful social task." *Behaviour Research and Therapy* 38, (12) (12/1): 1183-92.

Hollingworth, Harry L. 1935. *The psychology of the audience.* American psychology series. New York, Cincinnati etc.: American Book Company.

Horan, Roy. 2009. "The neuropsychological connection between creativity and meditation." *Creativity Research Journal* 21, (2): 199.

Jones, Amelia (1). 2006. *Self/image: Technology, representation and the contemporary subject.* New York, NY, US: Routledge/Taylor & Francis Group.

**Kabat-Zinn, Jon. 2005. *Wherever you go, there you are : Mindfulness meditation in everyday life.* New York: Hyperion.**

Kashdan, Todd B., Anjali Mishra, William E. Breen, and Jeffrey J. Froh. 2009. "Gender differences in gratitude: Examining appraisals, narratives, the willingness to express emotions, and changes in psychological needs." *Journal of Personality* 77, (3): 691-730.

Kitzmann, Andreas. 2003. "That different place: Documenting the self within online environments." *Biography* 26, (1) (Winter): 48.

Kluth, Elizabeth. 2006. "Among the audience." *The Economist.* April 20th, 2006.

Kushner, David. 2006. "Prime time for vlogs?" *Business 2.0* 7, (4) (May): 24.

Langer, Ellen J. 1989. *Mindfulness*. Reading, Mass.: Addison-Wesley Pub. Co.

**Leslie, Clare Walker, and Charles Edmund Roth. 2003; 2000. *Keeping a nature journal : Discover a whole new way of seeing the world around you*. 2nd ed. North Adams, MA: Storey Pub.**

Lindstrom, Madelene, Anna Staahl, Kristina Hook, Petra Sundstrom, Jarmo Laaksolathi, Marco Combetto, Alex Taylor, and Roberto Bresin. 2006. "Affective diary: Designing for bodily expressiveness and self-reflection." *Proceedings of the ACM SIGCHI conference Computer-Human Interaction* : 1037-42.

Lipton, Bruce H. 2008. *The biology of belief : Unleashing the power of consciousness, matter & miracles*. Carlsbad, CA: Hay House, Inc.

Mackenzie, Corey S., Ursula J. Wiprzycka, Lynn Hasher, and David Goldstein. 2008. "Seeing the glass half full: Optimistic expressive writing improves mental health among chronically stressed caregivers." *British Journal of Health Psychology* 13, (1) (Feb): 73-6.

**Madson, Patricia Ryan. 2005. *Improv wisdom : Don't prepare, just show up*. 1st ed. New York: Bell Tower.**

Meilach, Dona Z. 1993. *Looking great on video*. Homewood, Ill.: Business One Irwin.

Nalts, Kevin. 2008. "How to get popular on YouTube without any talent." *Will Video For Food, LLC.*

Nardi, Bonnie A., Diane J. Schiano, and Michelle Gumbrecht. 2004. "Blogging as social activity, or, would you let 900 million people read your diary?" Paper presented at *CSCW 2004: Proceedings of the 2004 ACM conference on Computer supported cooperative work*, Chicago, Illinois, USA.

**Nhat Hanh. 2008. *The world we have : A buddhist approach to peace and ecology*. Berkeley: Parallax Press.**

———. 1991. *Peace is every step : The path of mindfulness in everyday life*. New York, N.Y.: Bantam Books.

O. Mason, and Hargreaves I. 1 June 2001. "A qualitative study of mindfulness-based cognitive therapy for depression." *British Journal of Medical Psychology* 74, : 197,212(16).

Ohler, Jason. 2008. *Digital storytelling in the classroom: New media pathways to literacy, learning, and creativity*. Thousand Oaks, CA, US: Corwin Press.

Orr, Penelope P. 2006. "A documentary film project with first-year art therapy students." *The Arts in Psychotherapy* 33, (4): 281-7.

Palmer, Gareth. 2003. *Discipline and liberty : Television and governance*. Manchester, UK ; New York; New York: Manchester University Press; Distributed exclusively in the U.S.A. by Palgrave.

Parker, C., and S. Pfeiffer. 2005. "Video blogging: Content to the max." *Multimedia, IEEE* 12, (2): 4-8.

Parr, Clare J., and Sam Cartwright-Hatton. 2009. "Social anxiety in adolescents: The effect of video feedback on anxiety and the self-evaluation of performance." *Clinical Psychology & Psychotherapy* 16, (1): 46-54.

Pennebaker, James W. 1997. Opening up : *The healing power of expressing emotions*. New York: Guildford Press.

Puikkonen, Arto, Jonna Häkkilä, Rafael Ballagas, Jani Mäntyjärvi. 2009. "Practices in creating videos with mobile phones." Paper presented at *MobileHCI 2009: Proceedings of the 11th International Conference on Human-Computer Interaction with Mobile Devices and Services*, Bonn, Germany.

**Rainer, Tristine. 1978. *The new diary : How to use a journal for self-guidance and expanded creativity*. Los Angeles; New York: J. P. Tarcher; dist. by St. Martin's Press.**

Rapee, Ronald M., and Kim Hayman. 1996. "The effects of video feedback on the self-evaluation of performance." *Behaviour Research and Therapy* 34, (4) (4): 315-22.

Rodebaugh, Thomas L., and Dianne L. Chambless. 2002. "The effects of video feedback on self-perception of performance: A replication and extension." *Cognitive Therapy and Research* 26, (5) (10/01): 629-44.

Ryan, Paul. 1993. *Video mind, earth mind : Art, communications, and ecology*. Semiotics and the human sciences. Vol. 5. New York: P. Lang.

**Simmons, Annette. 2001. *The story factor : Secrets of influence from the art of storytelling*. New York: Basic Books.**

Sloan, Denise M., Brian P. Marx, Eva M. Epstein, and Jennifer L. Dobbs. 2008. "Expressive writing buffers against maladaptive rumination." *Emotion* 8, (2) (Apr): 302-6.

Smith, Jay. 2003. "On the air, unaware: Narcissism and transformation in the truman show." *Journal of the British Association of Psychotherapists* (BAP) 41, (2) (Jul): 152-8.

**Soneff, Sharon. 2008. *Art journals & creative healing : Restoring the spirit through self-expression*. Beverly, MA: Quarry Books.**

Thoreau, Henry David, and John C. Broderick. 1981. *Journal. The writings of Henry D. Thoreau*. Princeton, N.J.: Princeton University Press.

Tikka, Pia. 2004. "(Interactive) cinema as a model of mind." *Digital Creativity* 15, (1) (03): 14-7.

**Tolle, Eckhart. 2004. *The power of NOW : A guide to spiritual enlightenment*. Rev ed. Vancouver, B.C., Canada; Novato, Calif.: Namaste Pub.; New World Library.**

Triplett, Robert. 1983. *Stagefright : Letting it work for you*. Chicago: Nelson-Hall.

Turner, Graeme. 2006. "The mass production of celebrity: 'celetoids', reality TV and the 'demotic turn'." *International Journal of Cultural Studies* 9, (2) (June 1): 153-65.

Twenge, Jean M., and W. Keith Campbell. 2009. *The narcissism epidemic : Living in the age of entitlement*. New York: Free Press.

Valkanova, Yordanka, and Mike Watts. 2007. "Digital story telling in a science classroom: Reflective self-learning (RSL) in action." *Early Child Development* 177, (6-7) (Aug): 793-807.

van Dijck, José. 2007. *Mediated memories in the digital age*. Stanford University Press.

Vaynerchuk, Gary. 2009. *Crush it! : Why now is the time to cash in on your passion. 1st ed.* New York: HarperStudio.

**Verdi, Michael, Ryanne Hodson, Diana Weynand, and Shirley Craig. 2006. *Secrets of videoblogging*. Berkeley, Calif.: Peachpit.**

"Wesch - Anthropology Program at Kansas State University." 10/24/2009 <http://ksuanth.weebly.com/wesch.html>.

**Woods, Linda, and Karen Dinino. *Journal Revolution : Rise Up and Create! : Art Journals, Personal Manifestos, and Other Artistic Insurrections*. 1st ed. Cincinnati, Ohio: North Light Books, 2007.**

Williams, Redford B., and Virginia Parrott Williams. 1994; 1993. *Anger kills : Seventeen strategies for controlling the hostility that can harm your health*. HarperPerennial ed. New York: HarperCollins Publishers.

Williamson, Marianne. 1996. *A return to love : Reflections on the principles of a course in miracles*. New York: HarperCollins.

Yogo, Masao, and Shuji Fujihara. 2008. "Working memory capacity can be improved by expressive writing: A randomized experiment in a Japanese sample." *British Journal of Health Psychology* 13, (1) (Feb): 77-80.

# Index

## Symbols



## A



## B



## C



## D



## E



## F



## G

## H



## I



## J



## K



## L



## M



## N



## O



## P



## R

## S



## T



## U



## V



## W



## Y



## Z

Made in the USA
Monee, IL
08 November 2026

67971950R00122